You Can Sleep
in Your Car,

But You Can't Drive
Your House to Work

Andy!
Thank you for your
encouragement message
AKA 'ship it!'.
God Bless!
Senator Banks

YOU CAN SLEEP IN YOUR CAR,

But You Can't Drive Your House to Work

by SUTTON PARKS

RAGPICKER
PUBLISHING

Ragpicker Publishing

PO Box 682662
Franklin, TN 37068
© **2011 Sutton Parks**
www.suttonparks.com

For Larry A. and Father Gordon.

**Your time, counsel, love, wisdom and example
showed me how to live and saved me from myself.**

*"Constantly thank God. When suffering, thank God for
needing his comfort and love"*

—Fr. Gordon.

*"Our first thought should be for other people;
how we can best serve them"*

—Larry A.

ACKNOWLEDGMENTS

Words on a page can never express my gratitude for those who have loved, helped, encouraged and prayed for me. Hopefully I can pass on to others what I have been given so freely. Thank you Mom and Dad, Bob, Scott, Denise and Jennifer. I couldn't ask for a better family.

For Carla Theodore, Joanne Miller and Andrea Reynolds. Without your encouragement and wisdom this book would be just a collection of words. Without you, my dream of writing a book would have never come true. From the depth of my heart, thank you.

For Janelle Nobles from In HIS Image Productions, thank you for the remarkable cover photo. For Charles Sutherland of E.T. Lowe Publishing, thank you for your patience and guidance in providing an exceptional layout design.

For my mentors and friends. Forgive me for those I have missed. Here are a few:

Dan and Joanne Miller—a special thanks to you for your kindness, love and generosity. Without you I would have never had the courage to start writing this book.

For Larry A., Father Gordon, Zig Ziglar, Og Mandino, Phil and Carla Theodore, Justin Lukasavige, Kent Julian, Fred Mindermann, Chad Jeffers, Chadrick Black, Archie Winningham, David Shotwell, David Blue, "Cappo"(love ya man!), Rob Clinton, Joel Boggess, The Dierken's, Mike Dinwiddie, Tom Wurth, Kenny Horton, David Dutton, Dick and Judy Edelstein, "Goobs", Taylor Milam, Robert Stewart, Chris Prothro, Jim and Julie Rich, Ms. Sandy, Bobby Flake, Steve D., David Sappington, Buck Moorehead, Glen Kuykendall, Buddy Shula, Dr. Staten Medsker, Dr. Norman Vincent Peale, Missy Stauffer, Costco

Sue, Dave Werbeck, Keith Baxter, Dr. Dan Baker, Ashley and Nathan Logsdon, Randell Mark, Dr. Denis Waitley, Napolean Hill, Kevin Miller, Jared Angaza, Jack Canfield, Tim Ferriss, George Wolanske, Micro Arts (book cover), Doug Wead, Kirk Johnson, Bob Baker, Brent Green, Jeff Jones, Mandy Green and Janet.

SUMMER 2004

Is That All There Is?

"If that's all there is, my friend, then let's keep dancing, break out the booze and have a ball, if that's all, there is."

Is That All There Is?
By Peggy Lee, written by Mike Stoller and Jerry Leiber

A dark cloud seemed to engulf my body, from the top of my head to my toes. I felt I was suffocating from monotony. I grabbed my favorite Mason jar, filled it with cheap, red Chardonnay, and took a good, healthy gulp. This was not the kind of wine you buy to sip while gazing at the sunset on your friends' boat. This was the kind you buy in a box, for yourself. No sharing necessary. It's the kind of wine you drink to forget.

The air conditioner kicked on in my 2-year-old, 3-bedroom house in the brand-spanking new subdivision of Haynes Crossing. It was yet another humid Saturday in Tennessee, with temperatures reaching the low 90's. I stood unsteady on the beige carpet of my master bedroom, with the upgraded trey ceiling, walk-in closet, and ensuite bathroom. All the Venetian blinds were closed, keeping the light where it belonged, outside, far from the dark place I had entered. My roommate was out with his girlfriend

Lookin' at the world through the bottom of a glass, All I see is a man who's fading fast.

—Misery and Gin by Merle Haggard

3

> *"But I'm near the end and I just ain't got the time, oh no. And I'm wasted and I can't find my way home"*
>
> —**Can't Find My Way Home, Steve Winwood**

of the moment. Neighbors were busy taking kids to baseball games and out for burgers. My family was going about life in towns with names like Sidman Pennsylvania, and North Tonawanda New York. And I was alone.

The emotional crooning of Peggy Lee, along with several hours of drinking on an empty stomach, hit me like a sucker punch to the gut. I felt dark. That's the only way I can describe the feeling. *This is lonely,* I thought to myself, *and it will never change.* I hit repeat on the boombox and listened to the song again. I walked into my bathroom and reached into the tub to turn on the water. I held my hand under the faucet to make sure the temperature was right. *Is this really all there is?* I wondered.

I was on repeat. Work, get drunk, sleep, work, get drunk, sleep. It was Bill Murray's *Groundhog Day,* but not funny. I longed to have just two good days. Two days that are different, exciting, adventurous, anything! I truly felt I was in a deep rut and couldn't see a way out. Until I did see a way out, but that way wasn't pretty. *Why not save yourself all this future suffering?* I asked myself. *I was going to die someday anyway, why not just die now and avoid this loneliness? Nothing will ever change. I'm a loser.* These thoughts haunted me and I didn't know how to break the cycle.

Somewhere in the back of my messy closet I stored my hiking equipment. There was an old pocketknife in there that was given to me as a gift from my brother-in-law on the day he married my sister. I'd rarely used it since moving from the farm years earlier where I worked as a diesel mechanic. Now something was telling me I had a use for it.

The wine spread a sensation of warmth through my body as I took another big swig. The tub was filling up. I turned off the faucet, then stood up slowly and turned around to look at myself in the mirror. *You are a loser.* I said to the sad, desperate man in the reflection. "Let's break out the booze and have a ball," I drunkenly slurred along with Peggy Lee. Leaning against the beige colored Formica bathroom counter top I slid the knife up my arm following a vein.

Years earlier I had worked in a factory where a fellow told me about his experience as a volunteer fireman. He explained how to be successful when slashing your wrists in some sort of twisted conversation one day. "Cut up the vein, not across the wrist, for maximum blood loss," he said. "A cut across the wrist may heal before enough blood drains out."

But the blade of my old pocketknife wouldn't cut the skin. I pressed hard enough for it to hurt. Still nothing but a faint red mark. *Damn, I can't even do this right!* I complained to myself. I put the tip of the blade on the artery at my wrist and pressed down harder this time. It was just a small cut, hardly any blood. I couldn't puncture the main artery without causing myself more pain. And it was pain that I was trying to escape.

The reason I wanted to die was because I was in pain, emotional pain. So I picked what I thought would be a painless way to die. Just cut the vein, drink some wine, listen to music and fall asleep in the warm bathwater. But, the knife wouldn't cooperate with my seemingly easy plan.

That knife used to cut through anything like butter: bailing twine wrapped around a lawn mower blade, plastic weed trimmer line, automotive motor belts, anything. I never had to sharpen it. Now it was as dull as my head after three-quarters of a box of wine. *How much pain do you want to go through?* I asked myself.

> *As a child my family's menu consisted of two choices: take it or leave it.*
> —*Buddy Hackett*

I stopped and looked at the swollen, hazel eyes of the drunken man staring back at me in the mirror. A thought popped into my head: *Call Mike NOW!* (Mike was a friend who lived two doors down from me.)

This was not the kind of thought you need to mull over. It was an immediate call to action. I'm not sure where that thought came from, but something changed for me at that moment and I picked up the phone and dialed. Luckily for me, Mike answered. "Mike, can you come over right now?" I pleaded. He must have heard the urgency in my voice. "Sure." he said. I was temporarily saved from myself.

A Little Background

I grew up in North Tonawanda, NY, a suburb of Buffalo. I was the second youngest of five children. My father worked at an automotive factory that poured molten cast iron into molds for engine blocks. My mother watched and took care of us kids.

My father hated his job and let us know about it everyday, complaining of the "dusty, dirty foundry" he worked in. He grew up on a dairy farm in western Pennsylvania. My dad's hobbies were work and more work. We had the biggest garden on the block and heated our house with a wood stove from trees we knocked down and split. Each morning was a choice between sleeping in and getting yelled at. I usually chose the sleep which would always end up in a major argument with my father.

I was the lazy one. My two older brothers worked hard and carried most of the work load. My dad supervised. Some how I always got off easier than my brothers. I think they resented me for that.

Even though I hated doing chores for free I worked hard when it was a paying job. While in New York, I collected newspapers door to door and sold them to recycling companies that paid well at that time. I also had a paper route, sometimes two, and worked for a local farmer bailing hay in the summer, delivering it to the southern

> "I used to work in a fire hydrant factory. You couldn't park anywhere near the place."
>
> —Steven Wright

New York Amish farmers in winter. I had money in the bank, a new stereo, a go-cart and an electric guitar.

While working for the local farmer, I learned to like beer. I was paid $3 an hour, lunch, and all the Mountain Dew or beer I could drink. The first summer I would open a beer, take a sip and then hand it to my co-worker George. George was my hero. I was 13, he was 16. He had a beard, drove an old pickup truck and played lead guitar in a country music band on weekends. I wanted to be like George, but I hated the taste of beer. By the end of the summer I didn't mind the taste and I sure enjoyed how relaxed I felt after three or four cold beers. I also felt grown up.

As a teenager I started playing guitar and writing songs. My first guitar teacher taught me by the book. I was learning how to read music and play *Mary Had A Little Lamb*. I quit. I wanted to learn *Long Haired Country Boy* and *Freebird*. I found a teacher who would teach me only the songs I wanted to learn. I excelled. I couldn't wait to learn a new song and play it for my friends.

Back then I was always listening to the radio. It seemed like many of the songs I heard said the same things. When a new song came out I would try to guess the next lyric the singer was about to sing as I was listening to the song. It surprised my how many times I was right or close to it. *I could write these songs.* I thought. So I started writing songs and creating rhymes.

When I was 15 the foundry my dad worked at shut down, so my dad retired and moved us to an isolated farm in western Pennsylvania. On a three-mile stretch of road there were only six houses. From the driveway you could see only one other home on the distant hillside. There were no sidewalks, streetlights, neighbors, ice hockey, street hockey, pick up games of football, 7-11 stores or any other thing of interest for a 15-year-old city boy.

My older brothers and oldest sister had already moved out, so it was just my younger sister and parents who moved. I hated it. I missed my friends with whom I had grown up and shared so much of my life. I missed my grandma and my relatives.

I missed having money. Western Pennsylvania was the most economically depressed area of the country when we moved there in 1983. I couldn't find the kind of work I was able to do back in New York. I felt isolated, alone and powerless without my friends and any way to earn money.

When we moved, playing guitar, writing songs and going for long walks in the woods were the only things I was interested in, besides drinking beer.

After high school I went to Williamsport, Pennsylvania to learn Diesel Mechanics. I made the Dean's List the first year. Then I started hanging out with the party crowd. I would bring my guitar and play at parties. They would give me free beer. I dropped out after one semester of doing that.

I moved back to my parents' farm and struggled to find work. I worked as a diesel mechanic, then sold vacuum cleaners door to door, then on to health club sales and ended up selling family photography for Olan Mills Studios. I drove up and down the north east coast working out of churches and motels convincing people on the value of having a nice family portrait. One night while on the road I got really drunk and showed up late for an appointment with my manager. I decided it would be best just to quit, rather than try to explain myself. So I quit.

Around that time I had an opportunity to move back to Buffalo, New York, with my old friends. I had had enough of Pennsylvania so I moved. There I worked in a factory for a few years and tried to put myself through college at night. The demands of working at a factory and paying tuition were too much. I never took any ACT or SAT tests, so to gain admission they let me take one course at a time until I could build up some credits with a sufficient GPA so they could admit me. Without admissions I couldn't get a student loan, and without a student loan I couldn't continue to afford the tuition on my factory wages.

"I can't believe God put us on this earth to be ordinary".

—**Lou Holtz**

However in the coursework I did complete, I got all A's. I took micro and macro-economics, a creativity course, and some other class. I loved economics and was lucky to have excellent professors. Doing well built up some confidence in me that I could do more than be a human machine on an assembly line.

I hated that factory. Everyone there seemed stuck. Nobody liked it but the money was too good to quit. Not a lot of money, but just enough to keep you from leaving.

One Saturday morning I came in to work at 6 a.m. for some overtime. I was listening to motivational tapes on the way to work, trying to stay positive. My boss, a plus-size, balding man with a negative attitude, was standing at the time clock. "Good morning John!" I smiled as I approached the clock. "What's so fu&#ing good about it?" he replied. It was a tough place to stay optimistic.

After three years I finally got the courage to quit. I got into an argument with my foreman over breaks. He would give most people a break from the assembly line every hour to smoke. I didn't smoke, but had to go to the bathroom. He didn't give me a break that day. So I let him have it. By the time we were done arguing, six people were standing around in amusement as I yelled in his face that, "One of us is stupid, and I think it's you!"

He called over the union representative and we went into his office. I was written up. I was so pissed off. I put myself into a panic attack. My heart was racing, I was breathing as if I had just run a marathon. They asked me if I wanted to go to the hospital. I figured sure, let them spend some money if they're going to treat me this way. So they called a cab and sent me to Buffalo General Hospital. I just sat in the doctor's office until she sent me home. The factory paid for the cab but not the deductible on the medical bill. I felt it was a work-related illness and they should pay it. I filed a grievance with the union. One morning the union representative told me they couldn't help me with the case and I would have to pay the bill. I told a friend good-bye, grabbed my time card, punched out and left.

When I walked out I felt a weight lift from my shoulders. That place really sucked. I wound up back at a health club selling memberships and playing music at nights. I couldn't have been happier.

I moved to Nashville from Buffalo after taking the "rocking chair" test in 1995. In one of his books, motivational speaker Tony Robbins writes about imagining your life at age seventy. You are in a rocking chair on your porch thinking about your life. What do you wish you had done when you were younger? What risk do you wish you had taken when you were younger?

> *"All our dreams can come true, if we have the courage to pursue them".*
> —*Walt Disney*

I was playing music in nightclubs around Buffalo and loving every minute of it. I had also been writing songs since I was twelve and getting pretty good at it. I wanted nothing more than to travel the world and play music. I didn't care if I became famous, although I would have liked that. I really wanted to travel, write and sing my songs.

So I loaded up my car with everything I owned along with $500 cash and moved to Nashville. I slept on a friend's couch for the first month, got a job and sang at every amateur songwriter's night in town. I was living my dream.

I worked in a mailroom of music company, BMI. They promoted me to a computer operator in the data center. I went from visiting people everyday, dropping off their mail to working alone at night and getting home at midnight when all my friends were asleep. I became lonely and was no longer playing music with my friends, but I was making more money than I ever had. I thought I was being responsible and being upwardly mobile. Instead I was denying myself what I loved and digging my own grave.

Being a computer operator is similar to the job the cartoon character Homer Simpson holds. You sit in front of 20 computer monitors and, if something goes wrong, you call a computer programmer to fix it. It was a job to nowhere. Once I realized I had climbed to the top of the ladder in that position, I wanted out.

I have worked for some wonderful, competent, kind-hearted people in my life. This was not one of those times. My boss had a PhD in psychology (first sign of a troubled person?), had a career as a truck driver (do those two things even mix?) and was now a supervisor in Information Technology (IT). If anything went wrong, eventually the blame would fall on whichever operator was working at that time. I was convinced my job was meant to be a scapegoat for the incompetence of the managers and programmers. The good part is he never said anything to me about coming back from lunch drunk, so I guess he wasn't so bad.

We did get busy at times. We printed quarterly royalty checks for songwriters and when we did everyone was nervous because the checks had to be correct and on time.

One night they heavily loaded down my schedule. I was supposed to print the checks, bring the mainframe computer down and restart it for maintenance, run the regular nightly schedule and complete the work the first shift never got around to doing. I was alone that night and knew that was a recipe for disaster. Since the checks and nightly schedule were high priority, I completed them then sent the boss an email stating *I had no intention* of performing the first shift's work as well.

Well, that got me called to a meeting with the Vice President of the department and three managers. The VP was neutral, so it was one against three. I could have been 1 against 103 people because I was right. I brought with me a copy of my work schedule and job description. I gave each of them a copy and asked them if it was reasonable to put such a workload on a new operator and, if it wasn't, why didn't they call in another operator to help? The VP sided with me, but sent me to an email etiquette course, explaining that I need to be more careful wording my emails.

The managers were not happy with this decision and one of them later pulled me aside and said, "Off the record, you got away with one." He talked longer than I paid attention.

Six months later they moved a guy on third shift (12 a.m. to 8 a.m.) onto first shift (9 a.m. to 5p.m.). Then they put me on third shift, or they tried to. Third shift workers not only worked all night, they also worked every weekend. Tuesday and Wednesday were their days off instead of Saturday and Sunday.

A co-worker called me at home and told me about the change. Luckily I had time to think about it. I decided to quit, but not do anything that would get me arrested. In fact, I wanted to leave in a calm, classy manner without taking it personally.

When I arrived at work later that day, they told me about the change. I told them I agreed to work the second shift, not third. I calmly stated, "If you feel you need me on third shift, then I appreciate the six years of employment at BMI, however I quit." Then I handed them their security badge. The supervisor told me to wait and called in his boss . . . the one who threatened me.

I should have just ignored him and left. However, I was still an immature 36-year-old. The manager came in and sat down. He folded his arms and stared at the ground. His posture and arrogant tone of voice really set me off. He didn't say, "Why are you leaving?" or even, "Thank you for your service." In a cocky tone of voice he said only: "I need a note."

Well, my thoughts of leaving with dignity were never well thought out. *Does he know I'm thinking of whipping his ass and throwing it out the plate glass window?* I thought to myself.

Don't get arrested, just leave. Finally I had a "sane" thought. I straightened my shoulders, stood tall, stared directly at him and assertively said, "You can suck my dick!" Then I walked out.

Within two months I got a job in customer service for Verizon Wireless cell phones. I was paid to collect money on delinquent cell phone bills. The management was excellent and appreciative. It was like night and day compared to where I had come from. After a year I received a raise and a promotion. About that time I tried to quit drinking. Not drinking and being a bill collector became difficult for me. People hated when you called; they threatened you, and I took it

> *"What's money? A man is a success if he gets up in the morning and goes to bed at night and in between does what he wants to do."*
>
> —*Bob Dylan*

personally. I shouldn't have; but I did. Even though I loved my boss, Daryl, one day I just stopped showing up.

I was on my way to work the sunny day in May when I stopped at a Starbucks for some coffee. I sat down and read the *New York Times* story about a contractor in Iraq who was kidnapped by al-Qaida, had his head cut off with a sword and the video was posted on the Internet.

The man was close to my age, trying to earn some extra money for his family. I sat there thinking how tragic that story is and how shocked and saddened his family must feel. I might have gone to Iraq if I had the opportunity and experienced the same circumstances as he. *Instead, I'm alive at Starbucks,* I reflected.

Collecting cell phone bills seemed pretty insignificant to me in that moment, especially since I didn't enjoy it. I thought: *What do I really want to do? If this were my last day on earth, what would I do? Go hiking!,* I answered myself. So I went hiking. I had already used up all my sick and personal days for the year—and it was only May—so I didn't see any reason to call in. I just quit going in to work. That was May of 2004. I had purchased a new home two years prior to this and left myself no way to pay the mortgage without a job.

OCTOBER 2004

Every night I go to sleep The blues fall down like rain
Every night I go to sleep
The blues fall down like rain
Taking pills, cheap whiskey
Just to try to ease the pain

—Shot Gun Blues by Richard and Don Walsh
Performed by the Blues Brothers

Foreclosure

The night was fading into the red morning sky, illuminated by a half-round fiery sun rising in the distance. A misty fog half-covered the neighbors' Halloween decorations giving them an eerie appearance. My car rolled slowly into the suburban neighborhood in Spring Hill, where I lived. Stepping from my car to open the garage door, I heard the familiar sound of the morning songbirds singing, greeting another beautiful fall day. I pulled my gold, four-door, 1989 Dodge Dynasty into my two-car garage and shut the door.

> *"I had a friend who was a clown. When he died, all his friends went to the funeral in one car."*
> —**Steven Wright**

I switched off the engine and looked at my watch: 6:11 a.m. In less than five hours I was scheduled to play a song at the small Methodist church I attended regularly. There was no way I was going to make it. My eyes were heavy and bloodshot and my head just plain hurt. I walked into my kitchen, opened the refrigerator and looked for a beer. No beer. I checked the freezer. My roommate's stash of weed in the freezer was gone. This was not an ideal way to start a day, or end a night.

A letter written on legal stationary from my bank stared at me from the top of my kitchen stove. I didn't need to read it to know what it was. It read something like this:

On Monday, tomorrow, your home will be sold on the Maury County Courthouse steps in Columbia, TN, at a foreclosure auction.

Seeing that letter on the stove hit me hard and once again reminded me I was a loser.

I was thirty-seven years old. Thirty-seven years old with no job, a house in foreclosure, no money, a Dodge with 245,000 miles on it, a big fat headache, no beer, bourbon or weed. And now, I was about to miss this commitment to play and sing at church. *If that's not a loser, what is?* I thought to myself over and over again. I got myself into this mess and if I knew a way out of it I wouldn't be here in the first place.

I thought about playing at church that morning. My name would be in the bulletin, "Sutton Parks, musical ministry," just before the sermon. They would call my name and no one would get up from the pew. Silence. I knew I should go but there was no way I could. I was hung over from an all night bender, and smelled like stale Jack Daniels and campfire smoke. No hot shower or cologne will cover up this stench. The whiskey was in my pores. *What the hell is wrong with me?* I asked myself. *I can't do anything right.* My self-loathing was infinite.

I felt defeated and saw no realistic way out. There was no hope for me. Thirty-seven years of failure. I had to concede that I was not meant for this world. Life would always be a constant struggle. Whether I liked it or not, I just didn't have whatever it took to make it in life and enjoy it. I was dealt a pretty good hand of cards, being born in the USA during a prosperous economy with a good family life and still I failed.

I needed a way out of this daily struggle and frustration. Opportunities and dreams passed me by. I would sit and watch them disappear like a puffs of smoke: money, girlfriends, jobs, youth, and most importantly, hope, all disappeared for me. I was just getting by everyday and living paycheck to paycheck. And I was barely doing that.

I thought about jumping from the Natchez Trace Bridge just down the road from me. At 155 feet high I knew it would work. However, after extended contemplation, I decided that was not my way out.

They say right before you die everything slows down. If the fall took

> *"Remembering that you are going to die is the best way I know to avoid the trap of thinking you have something to lose. You are already naked. There is no reason not to follow your heart".*
>
> —*Steve Jobs*

two seconds and everything slowed down, I may have time to think. And what if, as soon as my feet left the bridge I had second thoughts: *Maybe it's not so bad. Maybe I should have tried 'this' or 'that'. Since I am going to die maybe I should have run up my credit cards and gone on a trip to Europe. Who cares about credit card debt, I'm going to kill myself anyway? Maybe I should have asked that girl out or written a book. Who cares about rejection? I'm going to kill myself. And maybe, just maybe, some of that would work. Who knows? Maybe that girl will say yes, maybe someone will read my book. Maybe I'll start to have some success. Maybe if I just go all out and take the risks I was afraid to make . . .*

And then SPLAT! Jumping off a bridge and then having time to change my mind on the way down was not how I wanted to spend the last moments of my life. There must be another way.

A neighbor I grew up with committed suicide a few years earlier. He shut his garage door and left his car running. He just fell asleep. That seemed to me to be the best way to leave this world. Just fall asleep. *Maybe I'm on to something here,* I thought. Falling asleep would be much easier than waking up and having to live another depressing day in my shoes. In a moment of utter despair, fatigue, loneliness, and heartbreaking pain, I made the final decision.

As I locked my closed garage door, I thought to myself, *I will never have to feel this way again! Finally, I will get some relief from this life I'm living. I cannot take it! If this is how it is going to be for the next thirty years of my life, then I'm checking out.*

Then I got in my car, shut the door, rolled the window down and started the engine.

As I sat there I wished I had a few beers and a joint. *That would help me fall asleep,* I thought to myself. The radio played a few songs and I eased my front seat back. I wasn't sure how long it would take for the carbon monoxide to put me to sleep but I had a half-tank of gas and I was sure that would be enough. I thought of all the problems I was finally going to escape. My thoughts were all positive . . . positive that I had finally made the right decision.

This is a much better excuse for missing church this morning than being hungover, I concluded. It doesn't make much sense now, but at the time it all seemed like a simple solution to a problem. In reality it was a permanent solution to a temporary problem. Saying, *I'm not going to make it to church to sing today folks because I'm in the process of killing myself* makes no sense. However my thoughts were completely out of whack and I was too deep in depression to recognize it.

I was so depressed I thought of suicide every day. I figured anyone who said they didn't think of suicide was lying about it. Everyone thinks of killing himself, I thought. I was afraid to tell anyone because I thought they would commit me to an asylum if I did. And then, locked up, I would want to kill myself even more.

I thought of the foreclosure the next morning. What better way to escape the embarrassment of losing your home than by killing yourself? *People would feel sorry for me rather than judge me and consider me a loser,* I surmised. In my whole life I have never known anyone who had lost his home. I have heard that it happens, but it was rare, as far as I knew. Losing my home proved once and for all I was a failure. Having a home was my outer shield; it meant I was a Regular Joe who was capable of holding a job and owning a home. It was the American Dream. But it was no longer a dream.

My house was validation that I was someone, that I was going somewhere in life and had arrived. I thought it ensured my standing in the community, and would be the great investment to help me jump to the next social class in life. I was a homeowner! What I refused to consider was the reality of a mortgage.

The reality was that the bank owned the house and I paid the interest and a tiny amount on the principal each month. I brought home

$1600 a month after taxes and my house payment was $1100. All but $100 of that was interest. Home values were not going up as fast as people said they would when I bought the home and neither did my income. My employer never gave me the promotion I thought I had earned.

> "Every great man, every successful man, no matter what the field of endeavor, has known the magic that lies in these words: every adversity has the seed of an equivalent or greater benefit"
>
> —W. Clement Stone

The salesman sold me the home with an interest rate that went up one percentage point each year for the first three years and then stayed the same from Year Three until Year Thirty. The reason behind this was to give upwardly mobile people like me a chance to take advantage of the great interest rates available. When the promotion comes along they should have no problem with the increase in interest for their new home. The bank was nice enough to lend me $144,000 for a home on my $26,000 a year income and I was dumb enough to sign on the line. Ultimately it was my decision to buy the house. And ultimately, it was my decision to kill myself.

Back in the garage, the motor was running and the radio was rockin'! However, I couldn't sleep! Did I have some kind of perverted version of insomnia? All I was doing was breathing in white smog, which had filled my garage, from the tailpipe of my car. I could hardly see the front end of the car. It was like driving in a thick fog or in a heavy northern snowfall. My plan had a fatal flaw in it (pun intended).

The problem was I owned a 1989 Dodge Dynasty with 245,000 miles on it that burned two quarts of oil with every tank of gas. It spit out white smoke like a cannon on the Fourth of July! When I drove down the street it left a trail of white smoke behind it as if it were a crop-dusting plane spreading insecticide over fields in the Midwest. And now somewhere in my garage was the carbon monoxide that would put me to sleep permanently. As luck would have it, the 20W-50 Valvoline haze pouring out from the exhaust pipe of my car had me gagging instead of nodding off to sleep. At that point, dying became more difficult than living... and I gave up.

To hell with this!, I thought. I wanted to fall asleep and die, nice and easy. Was that asking too much? I didn't want to be inhaling this filth, which left an oily taste in my mouth and burned my nostrils. I decided it would be easier to go into my bedroom and sleep than to continue breathing this foul air. I turned off the car engine and opened the garage door to let out the white smoke. I imagined my neighbors drinking their morning coffee, looking out their windows to see the smoke pouring from my garage, and calling the fire department. Luckily, that didn't happen or I probably would have been sent to the psychiatric ward. I went to my bedroom, collapsed in a heap on my bed and fell asleep at last.

I never heard from anyone at the church I was to play at that morning. A few weeks later I sheepishly went back and nobody mentioned it. I was glad they didn't.

Waiting

On Monday morning, my home was sold on the courthouse steps. I didn't receive any phone calls or notifications except for the letter that was on my stove.

I didn't move out though. I had heard from a friend who dealt in the foreclosure market that banks generally wait three months after the sale to take possession of the home. *Ah, three months free rent!* I thought.

But it was even better than that. My friend also said that the bank usually sends a representative to the property and if anyone is living there, they offer him or her some money to move out. Sometimes one thousand dollars or more!

OK, I can work with that. Once the bank gives me a check I can use that money to get into an apartment, my mind excitedly plotted. I would have a chance to start over again. All I had to do was wait for the guy from the bank to show up and write me a check.

When I moved into the house I had enough money to pay the mortgage and utilities, just the essentials. I had no furniture other than a queen-size bed my parents gave me as a gift. Luckily my roommate had a brown leather couch, an oversized Lazy Boy recliner, a TV stand and a new TV. The house came equipped with a new stove, refrigerator and microwave. What else did a single man need?

Of course my roommate moved out before the house was foreclosed on, so I was living in a home that

> *"How much of human life is lost in waiting?"*
>
> —*Ralph Waldo Emerson*

22

was practically empty. He saw the end coming and didn't like what he saw.

When I originally found out about the foreclosure, I sold a trailer load of my belongings to a friend who ran a booth at a local flea market on the weekends. My friend Tom had a box trailer and offered to help me. We loaded up my new mattress and box spring, the round kitchen table and chairs I bought at a thrift store, and

> *"I will love the light for it shows me the way, yet I will endure the darkness because it shows me the stars."*
>
> —*Og Mandino*

my tent. Anything else I owned of value was loaded as well. I figured if I had to move, I wanted to travel light until I found a place to settle. I received $110 dollars for a trailer load of stuff. It may not have been a lot of money, but I was broke and needed the money more than the stuff I sold.

On the way home Tom wouldn't let me buy him any gas to compensate and show him my appreciation. "Do you want to stop at the Pub and have a beer?," he asked. At that time I was trying to quit drinking and was attending 12-step meetings. Having been introduced to a 12-step program for a brief time in the early 90s, I left them because I didn't want to quit drinking. As my depression and financial problems increased I had started going back to the meetings at the end of 2003 because I was becoming so depressed and tired of living. I wanted things to get better with minimal effort on my part. I wasn't working the written program, just going to meetings and drinking coffee. Five months was the longest I went without drinking, but I smoked weed to help me keep off the sauce during that period. As my troubles mounted it became increasingly tough for me to go a week without drinking.

So I declined Tom's offer at first. But then I thought, *Since he won't take any gas money, it would be selfish of me not to buy him a meal and a beer.* So, at the gas station, after he filled up I said, "Hey Tom, let me buy you a beer and lunch for helping me out."

Well, Tom wasn't one to deny a friend's act of gratitude, especially when it involved a little Jack Daniels. We pulled into the SideTrack Pub

> *"We decide our own destiny. We always do."*
> —Og Mandino

in Spring Hill, and entered the dimly lit bar. As we entered, cigarette smoke filled our nostrils. Six men sitting at the bar looked over to see who was coming in. The jukebox was playing *I Love This Bar* by Toby Keith, and the pretty bartender with the low-cut blouse smiled at us.

It took a few seconds for our eyes to adjust from the sunlight to the barroom. Once they did, to my shock, I noticed a man sitting at the corner of the bar who had spoken at a 12-step meeting the day before! I didn't want him to see me because he would think that I was drinking. "Let's grab a table," I told Tom. I sat down with my back turned to the man at the bar. I wondered if he was drinking. Maybe he was just having lunch? I didn't know but I was pretty sure he didn't recognize me.

Tom and I ordered lunch. While we waited for our food to be prepared, he had a Jack Daniels on the rocks. In the traditional western Pennsylvania fashion I had a boilermaker. For those of you who are unfamiliar, this is a shot of whiskey and a beer to chase it down.

Four hours later, it was time for Tom to get home. I asked for the check. Shiiiiit!! The check was $75. Add on a $15 tip and that makes a total of $90.

Here is where my fourth grade arithmetic skills come in handy. Out of desperation for a few dollars I sold a bunch of stuff. I made $110 minus $90 for expenses (beer, whiskey, and bar food). That gave me a net of $20. Sadly, I had sold a trailer load of my possessions for $20. Once again, it was my own fault.

Tom lived just down the street from me. So we got in his truck with the trailer attached and started for home. "Tom, can we stop at the liquor store on the way?" I figured since I already spent most of the money I made getting wasted, I might as well get really wasted.

When I got home, I did just that. I continued getting drunk. Not for just that night, but for the next three months! I had no rent to pay.

My gas was turned off. (I thought I was moving so I had them turn it off. They wanted a $300 deposit to turn it back on.) My only bills were an electric utility bill and my cell phone bill.

Not having natural gas was a problem. Gas heated my stove, hot water tank, and my home. A friend lent me an electric radiator and I owned a small ceramic heater. I tried taking cold showers but as the weather got colder and the ground froze, the water coming into my house became frigid. I thought I could use my mind to overcome the freezing water coming out of the showerhead but I was wrong.

So, I found a creative solution. I borrowed a hot plate and would boil a frying pan of water on it. (My roommate owned all the cookware and took that with him when he moved out. So a frying pan was my biggest container to boil water.)

I would toss the hot water from the frying pan into the tub along with the cold water in the tub pouring from the faucet. I also used a coffee pot. I didn't put any coffee or filter in it, of course, and poured the water into the reservoir of the coffee pot, let it cycle and come out hot into the glass pot. Then I would dump that into the tub. It would take a minimum of 25 minutes to have enough lukewarm water to

"True happiness is to understand our duties toward God and man; to enjoy the present without anxious dependence upon the future; not to amuse ourselves with either hopes or fears but to rest satisfied with what we have, which is abundantly sufficient, for he that is so wants nothing."

—Seneca

bathe myself in. Still, it was better than a cold shower and it gave me something to do to kill some time.

My electric heaters had the capability to warm only my bedroom. I had to keep my bedroom door shut to keep the heat in. On a cold night, as when it hit 15 degrees, it would still be very cold in my room. I would have both heaters going all night and wear a wool beanie hat, wool socks, a couple of t-shirts and a sweater just to keep warm in an old sleeping bag. Thank God I had alcohol.

There wasn't much for me to do. A friend who had a construction business would give me work from time to time painting and laying ceramic tile. I used the money to keep the lights on, eat, and drink Jack Daniels and Natural Ice Beer.

My friends would visit, but they stopped inviting me to go to bars with them since they knew they would have to buy. If they were just going to the store they would stop by and give me a ride to the liquor store. They knew I would most likely need another half pint or twelve-pack, and that I shouldn't be driving.

Someone gave me an old TV with rabbit ears and I hooked it up inside my bedroom so I had some form of entertainment. In addition to the TV and heaters, I had a chair, a Therm-a-Rest® air mattress, and my acoustic guitar in my room. That was it. Getting drunk and watching the four channels on my TV consumed my life when I wasn't working or sleeping. I would also play and sing a few songs on my guitar.

And that leads me back to living in a foreclosed home. In November my old Dodge finally died. I was driving home from a 12-step meeting, heard a clunk, and the motor stopped. Coming from a background in mechanics, along with the fact that it had 248,000 miles on it, I knew the motor was shot. I called a friend for a ride, emptied out my car, and then called a junkyard and told them if they would pick it up, they could have it.

Not having a car is a problem. A big problem. There's an old song-writer saying, "You can sleep in your car, but you can't drive your house to work." I got lucky. My friend, Fred, knew a couple who was selling a dark gray, four-door, 1992, Chrysler New Yorker with 140,000 miles for $850! The front end was banged up from a crash and it needed a headlight. There were a few minor problems as well but it started up and gave a smooth ride. My parents came through with a loan and after a couple weeks of being stranded with no transportation, I was back in the saddle.

For those couple of weeks that I didn't have a car I had a great excuse to drink, all day, every day. What else was there to do?

I remember getting drunk and watching Oprah give everyone in the audience a brand new Pontiac G6. I cried. There was something about the hope it gave me: The hope of being rescued from my trials by someone or some twist of fate. (I'm guessing I watched a replay, because the show originally aired in September, and I watched it sometime over the winter months).

As the days wore on I fell deeper into despair. The only thing worse than having your home foreclosed and having to move is waiting for it all to happen. "Do the thing you fear the most and the death of fear is certain," said Thoreau. But I was still trying to hold on. I wouldn't let go and move on. This was an extremely unhealthy place to be. Nothing gets better when you can't move forward. I was stuck.

One day it struck me that no one was going to save me. There wouldn't be any winning lottery ticket, no check in the mail, and nobody really gave a shit about me. I felt like a neglected three-year-old child who just wanted his mommy's attention. Can life get any lonelier than this?

Between sips of cheap beer and commercials I came to terms with the fact that I was born alone and I will die alone. People are too busy with their own lives to baby-sit a grown man. There is no safety net. Life will let you fall hard on your ass and that is that. There may not be anyone there to help you get up.

It's a difficult feeling to describe. I learned that people will give up on you. Sometimes they *should*, at least in my case. Actions have consequences and sometimes

"Every new beginning comes from some other beginning's end".
—Closing Time, Semisonic

a life going down the drain is too hard to stop and can't be stopped by anyone else. I had to want things to get better: me, myself and I. No one else was going to do it for me.

I realized that if I lived, the day would come when I would have to start all over again and rebuild. And it would be up to me whether I failed or succeeded.

I was in no hurry though. As long as I lived in that house rent-free, I thought I might as well get drunk. I was living one day at a time. Being drunk helped me escape some of my feelings and pain. Nothing really changed; drinking to excess was just my way of easing the emotional burden I was under.

The man from the bank with the checkbook never showed up. Looking back, I imagine he stopped at the house, looked inside and saw no furniture and no proof of anyone living there and left. He figured it was already vacant.

Someone did stop by though. The Maury County Sheriff paid me a visit one afternoon while I was drinking a beer watching *Days of Our Lives*. He said he didn't think anyone was living inside and was stopping by to post a notice in case there was. He told me to be out by January 18th. I promised him I would and he left. Of course, most people would have already moved on and most people would certainly have moved after the sheriff orders them to. Not me. I was going to stay on this free ride as long as possible. It gave me another excuse to get drunk.

JANUARY 18, 2005

Gotta Go, Rock 'n' Roll

Do not get drunk on wine which leads to debauchery; instead be filled with the spirit.

— Ephesians 5:18

I thought I heard something… a faint knock on my front door. I kept my eyes shut and fought to get back to sleep. I figured whoever it was would go away. Again I heard the knocking but a little louder this time. I opened my eyes and stared at the white trey ceiling.

I was lying on top of my air mattress on the floor of my master bedroom. In the corner the TV was still on. My dirty clothes were thrown all over the floor and I heard the fan from the ceramic heater humming. That was probably the sheriff at my front door! I had to get up.

I had promised that I would be out that morning by 9 a.m. and I had meant it. Most of my belongings were already moved to a 10 x

Early this morning, when you knocked upon my door
Early this morning, oooo, when you knocked upon my door
And I said, "hello Satan, I believe it's time to go"
                    —Me and the Devil Blues, Robert Johnson

10 storage unit I rented down the street. I had planned on waking up at 6 a.m., figuring out where to go while I emptied the remains of the house. Instead, I got drunk and high that night at my neighbor's house and stumbled in at 4 a.m.

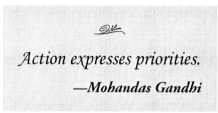

Action expresses priorities.

—Mohandas Gandhi

I jumped up and yelled down the hallway, "I'll be there in a minute!"

I threw on some clothes and ran across the hardwood flooring in the hallway to my front door. I opened the door and two guys were standing there holding black plastic Hefty bags. They looked shocked to see me. They were there to clean the house of any belongings I had. "Please give me a couple minutes and I'll get my stuff out of here right now. I just have a few things left," I exclaimed. As they walked away one of them picked up his cell phone. I started throwing everything I could into the moving boxes I had scattered throughout my bedroom.

I frantically called my friend Chris who lived down the street from me. "Chris can you bring your truck over, really quick?" Reliable as a Timex, Chris was there.

Then the sheriff showed up. I heard his footsteps down the hallway coming towards me. His gray hair peeked out of his sheriff's hat. The shiny black holster that held his pistol swayed around the side his big belly. "What are you doing here?" he said in a thick southern drawl. "I'm sorry," I pleaded, "I know I said I would be out of here but I just need a few minutes more." The sheriff frowned and gazed at me from beneath the brim of his hat. He looked both annoyed and irritated.

The two men with the black plastic Hefty bags came back in and went to work. I could hear my kitchen cabinets opening and glass banging together. Everything in the kitchen was being thrown into the bags and hauled out to the street curb for the garbage man. The dishes smashed, the spices bumped, and the silverware clattered. They weren't waiting for me anymore.

I threw my toothbrush and all my toiletries into a bag. I grabbed my guitar and took it out to the truck. My sleeping bag, coffee maker, clean and dirty clothes, were all loaded into my car. I left the TV, though. It

> *Being unwanted, unloved, uncared for, forgotten by everybody, I think that is a much greater hunger, a much greater poverty than the person who has nothing to eat.*
>
> *– Mother Teresa*

was just a cheap one given to me and why store something you're not going to use?

I filled Chris's white mini pick up truck and I filled my car with what was left. It is amazing how much stuff can fit into a house and yet the house still looks empty. I didn't realize how much junk I had stored in closets, the garage, and in the cabinets. The pile of my belongings at the curb was getting impressive. The garbage men won't be happy.

Black plastic bags lined the street, along with a workout bench, weights, TV, chairs, and anything else I didn't have room for. I looked at the garbage pile to see if there was anything I wanted. There were cooking spices, dishes, cups, coffee cups, frying pans, and silverware. I was so frustrated, I thought: *To hell with it all!* The cost of storing most of the junk would be more that it is worth. Besides, what was I going to do with it anyway?

As I was finishing loading up my car the sheriff walked up to my front door and taped a notice on the door. Then he came back to me and said in a very stern voice, "You are not allowed on this property anymore. If you come onto this property you will be arrested."

Well, that pissed me off! Everything I owned was out on the curb, my house had been foreclosed and I had nowhere to go. Now he was threatening me with arrest for trespassing. With fire I yelled back, "Why the hell would I want to come back here? I already know that and you don't have to threaten me!" I stepped towards him. He walked up to me and with a firm, angry voice said, "If you want to be an asshole I can take you to downtown Columbia right now and put you in jail."

Something told me to shut my mouth and I stopped for a minute. I realized I could really make things worse if I kept talking. So I apologized to him and just said, "You know, I'm under a lot of stress right now with all this going on and I'm sorry." He said to me, "I'm under a lot of stress, too." Again, that pissed me off. I thought: *Really, you're under a lot of stress? You have a gun on your holster, a job, a home, and a family. How much stress are you really under?* However, I bit my lip on that one. As Mom always said, sometimes it is best to be silent.

I'm sure he smelled some alcohol on my breath from the night before and I'm lucky he didn't give me a DUI for driving off in my car. But I got in and took off down the road with Chris following me in his truck. I looked in my rear view mirror and saw the wreckage of my life lying by the curb.

God Don't Make Junk

Later that morning I called my friend Fred who had just bought an old pig farm on the outside of town. He had dreams of turning it into a winery. There was an old farmhouse on the property that a bachelor had lived in for forty years. It served as the office of the yet-to-be-established winery. Fred once mentioned that I could stay in the house for a short while if I needed to. That was like hitting gold! I had a place to stay and a base of operations to start rebuilding my life.

The farmhouse was a one-story, two-bedroom home with a bathroom, living room and kitchen. It was built in the 1940s and looked it. There were a couple of mice running around but I don't think I bothered them much. It sat on 25 acres of rolling Tennessee farmland. A small pond, a run-down garage and open fields surrounded the home.

I only brought the necessities with me: toothbrush, guitar, some books and some clothes. It was temporary and I didn't want to take this chance for granted. I stayed there for ten days.

I picked up some work that week helping a friend, Randy from a 12-step meeting I attended, remodel a home making $9 per hour. I was desperate, broken and scared. I had no idea how I was going to make it through this mess I had made. I knew I had to do things differently, somehow connect with God and find some inspiration. Luckily this old pig farm out in the country was the perfect place for that.

> *"Every man dies. Not every man really lives"*
>
> —*William Wallace*

Behind the house was a steep hill with a trail up to the top. From the top, the view was spectacular. You could see the green, rolling Tennessee hills lined with trees. I made it a point to walk to the top every evening and bask in the winter sunset. I watched the clouds pass over the blue sky and spotted an occasional deer feeding on the grass or wild turkey walking at the edge of the woods. It was majestic and calming. I would say a few prayers and ask God for help with my life.

One day I was frustrated from working as I walked up to the top of the hill. The day was cloudy but the sun still shone through as it began to set in the horizon. I walked over the top, down the other side and back up. As I reached the top again I dropped to my knees and started crying and praying. A cool breeze blew across my face and I heard the wind whistle across my ears.

On my knees with my hands clenched together I was silent. I felt something inside of me appear, like a message. I didn't know where it came from and I believed then and I still believe now it was a message that God placed in my heart. The message was:

Picasso was a great artist, Stradivarius was a great violin maker, Beethoven was a great composer. They were all masters at their work. They were masters, but yet I made them. I am the maker of masters and I made you too! You were made by the same hand that made Beethoven, Stradivarius and Picasso. You were made by a Master Craftsman! And this Master Craftsman doesn't make junk. I don't have a scrap pile. Everything I make is a miracle.

(Later I re-read an Og Mandino book that had this line in it.)

Tears streamed down my cheek as I went into a moment of extreme gratitude. I thanked God for making me and thanked him for the challenges I faced. It was a very serene and beautiful moment. Then I stood up and walked back down to the house and went to bed.

> *"Success is going from failure to failure without a loss of enthusiasm"*
>
> —**Winston Churchill**

A few days later I got a call from Fred. He and his partners had hired a manager for the winery and I had to move out of the farmhouse to make room for the manager. I knew it was a temporary fix and I was grateful for what time I was given.

Now, however, I was back where I started . . . homeless.

My Last Drink

Sunday morning, the day before I had to move, I went to a church. Later that night I attended a bible study class. On my way to bible study I got a call from Tom. He asked me if I wanted to hang out at a pub in Spring Hill. He said he just wanted to talk and catch up. At first I declined the invitation. However, after bible study I changed my mind. I could just drink O'Doul's and still feel like I fit into the bar environment with my friends. So I called him up and we arrange to meet at the SideTrack Pub. I was back on the wagon, but that was about to be side-tracked as well.

I parked, walked in and sat on a stool at the bar. The bartender recognized me as a regular, gave me a smile and said, "Hey Sutton!" I smiled and replied, "Hi Candace. Can I have an O'Doul's?" O'Doul's, a non-alcoholic beer, would allow me to fit in at a bar yet not get drunk. Candace said, "Sure," walked away and came back. She placed a tall glass of Killian's draft in front of me. The white foam on

> *"The delusion that we are like other people, or presently may be, has to be smashed. We alcoholics are men and women who have lost the ability to control our drinking. We know that no real alcoholic ever recovers control"*
>
> —*p. 30 Alcoholics Anonymous*

top spilled over the side and slid down its curves along the icy condensation on the side of the glass.

A good bartender knows what their regular customers drink. I was a regular at that bar. I called it my home bar. Candace knew I liked to drink Killian's draft, get drunk, stare at her boobs and tip accordingly.

Three people sitting next to me said to the bartender, "He ordered an O'Doul's! That's not what he ordered!" "Did you order an O'Doul's, Sutton?" "I can take it back," Candace softly said. I watched the bubbles of air float to the top of the glass through the friendly, golden, smooth liquid. I had been sober for almost a week. The first thought that came into my mind was: *This must be God's Will.* It's funny how any behavior can be justified with a little thought. "No, that's OK, Candace".

I wish I could say that I drank that beer because I was nervous about having to move again or I was depressed and frustrated. That would be a logical explanation that anyone could understand. The fact is I felt fine that day. I was calm and comfortable. Yet once that beer was in front of me and I had a second to think about it, I couldn't see any reason not to drink it. I thought it would be fun to catch a buzz. There was no other reason. I had to learn that *attending* 12-step meetings is different than *working* a 12-step program. The meetings require no action. I would just sit down and drink coffee. When I did that I ended up drunk, again, because I couldn't resist. That's why it's called a drinking problem. If I had been able to just resist, it wouldn't be a problem.

"If, when you honestly want to, you find you cannot quit entirely, or if when drinking, you have little control over the amount you take, you are probably alcoholic"

—*p. 44 Alcoholics Anonymous*

That was all I said to Candace. There must have been something in that beer. It tasted so good I had to order another. My friend Tom likes to drink Jack Daniels. It's a bonding moment between friends when you order a shot, make a toast and drink it. Not one to decline an offer of friendship, Tom and I bonded over several shots of Jack Daniels, while I held my breath and chased them down with Killian's Red. I never liked the taste of the first few shots of Jack Daniels but I loved the effect! From there we switched to several different drinks. By the end of the night we were drinking some type of martinis. Stirred, not shaken.

When we left the bar, Tom offered to put me up for the night. Getting to his house was a different matter. It was one of those situations where the person who was the least drunk was going to drive. I offered to drive but Tom always liked to drive and he convinced me that he was in better shape than I was. He wasn't. The whole way back to his place I wished I was driving because he was swerving all over the road. That almost sobered me up right there, but not quite.

We got back to his house and I found a little bit of weed and I rolled it up in the paper receipt I got from my bar tab. I smoked it and slept in Tom's upstairs bonus room on a futon.

The next day I woke up feeling sick and tired. All I wanted to do was go back to sleep. But it was Monday and I promised to be out of the farmhouse that day. I loaded up all my belongings, cleaned up the farmhouse, and left. I went to my 10 x 10 storage unit. I got a change of clothes and got some camping equipment. At that point I had a plan.

Goin' Campin'

I once had a dream of walking the Appalachian Trail. I read several books on the subject and realized many people sleep outside in tents throughout the winter. So that was my stoic plan. There's a local state park called Henry Horton State Park, which is probably 35-40 minutes from Franklin. It cost $7 a night to rent a campsite. I figured that to be $210 a month. That is cheap living and that is just what I needed at that time. Even though it was February first, the price made the prospect of sleeping outside in the winter worthwhile. If it got too cold I would just move from my tent to my car, start it up, turn on the heat and sleep in my car that night. All I had to do was pull into the park and register for a campsite.

As I drove out to Henry Horton State Park I felt at ease. Finally I can settle in and get started rebuilding my life. I turned right onto the entrance road of the park and noticed a sign by the campsites that read, "Closed For The Winter." Well that shot right through my plans. I really didn't know what to do at that point. I prayed and asked God for help. I hadn't learned yet that God wants me to pray with my feet by doing something, as opposed to sitting around waiting for Him to answer my desperate prayers.

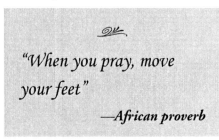

"When you pray, move your feet"

—*African proverb*

Hung over, tired and discouraged, I decided to go for a walk in the woods on one of the hiking trails. The sun was fighting through the misty morning fog as it lifted. While I walked around I approached the restrooms and they were

Life is like an ice-cream cone, you have to lick it one day at a time"
—*Charles M. Schulz*

closed for the winter as well. I guess this glamorous winter camping idea included tending to one's business outside. That's when it struck me: I am homeless.

afterwards, I walked over to a picnic bench, lay down on my back and looked up at the sky. I watched the wispy white clouds drift by and wondered what to do. I remembered that there was a 12 o'clock meeting for a 12-step group at a church in Franklin.

The Final Surrender

I got back in my car and I drove the 33 miles down I-65 South to the meeting. It was in the basement of an old church at the center of town. I approached the outside entrance passing the smokers standing outside, and walked down 12 cement steps. A faded green door with a cheap metal handle on it opened to the basement.

Inside were paper-brown colored metal chairs, a gray floor with chipped paint, and low florescent lighting. Along the wall was a table with a 4 top Bunn coffee maker filled with fresh coffee and a can of Oreo cookies sitting next to it. *Hey, free cookies and coffee? I'm in,* I thought. I grabbed a Styrofoam cup of hot coffee and a handful of cookies and sat down in the front row.

This wasn't my first 12-step meeting. For the last twelve months I had been coming and going. At the end of the meeting they give out white poker chips. They call them surrender chips. You are supposed to pick one up if you have had a drink recently and want to start over. They would tell me, "If you feel like drinking, just put that white chip in your mouth." I thought the chip would get in the way of my drinking so I never tried it. The stupid white chip never kept me sober.

"Contantly thank God. When suffering, thank God for needing his comfort and love"

—Fr. Gordon

They say the definition of insanity is doing the same thing over and over expecting different results. I had shit

42

> *"Look, if you had one shot, or one opportunity*
> *To seize everything you ever wanted in one moment*
> *Would you capture it or just let it slip?"*
>
> —*Lose Yourself, Eminem*

load of those white poker chips that I had picked up in previous meetings. So this time I didn't pick up a chip at the end of the meeting. (However, I did start carrying around a white chip in my front pocket from my stash, just as a reminder.)

I make light of it now, but I was scared at the time. Just because a bunch of people said they could live sober and change their lives around didn't mean I could. I had failed at many things other people succeeded at: network marketing businesses, weight loss plans, college plans, musical dreams. I failed at them all when others succeeded. As miserable and hopeless as I felt, I wouldn't let myself cry that day. I had cried before in meetings like this, but I had to accept my life as it was and get on with it. I came to that meeting for just one thing.

All I wanted was one day. One day sober. Give me one day sober. If I could get one day then I knew I could get two. I would just have to repeat that one day. Eventually I would have a week and I would just have to repeat that week to have two weeks. I figured if I could get one month sober, my mind would start to clear up. But it all starts with one day. Hence the saying, "One day at a time."

I walked out of the meeting feeling encouraged. There is something about hearing how others have solved their problems that gave me hope. I still had plenty of problems but having some hope lifted my spirits a bit. Now all I needed was a place to stay.

The TA Truckstop
(TravelCenters of America)

After that meeting, I had to figure out where I was going to sleep. Some friends offered me their couches, basements and spare bedrooms, but for some reason I didn't want to accept their offers. I needed a change. I also thought they may not be the best influence, as they were still living the partying lifestyle. If I was going to start over again, I knew I would have to start doing things differently.

I started brainstorming places where I could stay. By brainstorming, I mean worrying. As it got later in the day I thought to myself: *Well, if worse comes to worse, I could sleep in my car.* Then I thought: *Well I need a place that's safe to park my car. Maybe I could park it on the winery property somewhere.* But I didn't know if the owners would like a homeless guy parking on their land all night. Plus it was winter and there was a lot of mud. My car might get stuck, so I abandoned that idea.

"When your faith gets weak, start thanking God for anything and everything."

—**Father Gordon Walker**

I thought if I parked along the street the cops might come and harass me. It seemed a good idea not to park my car in a spot that would draw attention. Most municipalities prefer their citizens to sleep inside a house or hotel.

Then I thought that truck

stop on I-65 south, at the Peytonsville Road exit, just outside of Franklin. *That would work for one night*, I contemplated. *It should be safe and no one should bother me there.*

So at 10 p.m. that night I drove the 10 miles from Franklin to the truck stop. Pulling into the parking lot I drove to the right, where all the big rigs were. That's all I saw parked for the night; big rigs. I assumed a car would be out of place. I drove to the other side of the parking lot. On the outside perimeter, surrounding the gas pumps and restaurant, were more

> *"If you are going to approach God, you must be willing to accept mystery."*
> —**Father Gordon Walker**

parking spots. All the way in the back, in the darkest spot I could find, I backed my car between the two white parking lines.

High above the parking lot were several bright spotlights that lit up the parking lot. Luckily I happened to have one of those sunshades that you use in the summertime to keep the sun from heating up your car or destroying your dashboard. I pulled the sunshade out from my trunk along with my sleeping bag, pillow and toiletry bag. *This will also give me some privacy*, I thought, as I placed the sunshade over my windshield.

Next I grabbed my vanity bag, put on a ball cap to disguise myself as a trucker and walked across the parking lot and into the truck stop. I noticed a bathroom on the first floor and some wooden stairs going up to a second floor. I decided to see what was upstairs. As I walked up, I noticed several truckers sitting around a big screen TV watching basketball. Another trucker was seated at a table talking on his phone. A hallway at the top of the stairs led to some showers and a bathroom.

The showers were $10 unless you bought 100 gallons of diesel fuel. Ten dollars times thirty days a month equals three hundred dollars a month. I decided I couldn't afford to shower there.

However the bathroom upstairs was fairly clean. I laid my toiletry bag on the counter, brushed my teeth and washed my face. *This isn't like home, but it isn't so bad*, I concluded. Then I walked back downstairs, across the parking lot to my car.

The front driver's side seat of my car was broken. The back slid all the way into the back seat. Weeks earlier I placed a large, blue plastic storage box filled with books behind it so I could drive with the seat upright. Now it wouldn't recline back. So when I got to my car, I got into the passenger side.

Then I locked the doors. The sunshade blocked out most of the parking lot lights and gave me some privacy. I started the car and turned on the heat full blast. I took my boots off and put a second pair of wool socks over my socks. Next I put on a beanie winter cap to keep my head warm. I added a sweatshirt, a blanket and my sleeping bag.

Once the car got toasty I shut it off. I eased the passenger seat as far back as it would go. Then I closed my eyes and said, "Thank you God for a sober day," followed by the *Our Father*. I waited to fall asleep.

You don't sleep in your car. It is more like taking several naps waking up in between. The car would get freezing cold. The temperature outside dropped to 17 degrees that night. I was trying so hard to sleep I didn't want to open my eyes but it got so cold inside the car that I couldn't sleep. I felt as though I was literally freezing. I forced my eyes open and turned the keys in the ignition to start the frosty car. The motor roared to life. I waited for the heat. Once the inside of my car nice and toasty again I shut the engine off. Once again I tried to sleep. I couldn't sleep so I just lay there and waited for the sun to come up.

> "Such as are your habitual thoughts, such also will be the character of your mind; for the soul is dyed by the thoughts."
>
> —*Marcus Aurelius*

I decided I had to start moving when I had to pee! I couldn't hold it any longer. I ran across the frozen parking lot, used the bathroom, washed my face and brushed my teeth. Just like a trucker, except without the truck, the job and the family waiting at home.

I kept a few books in my car: a bible, a devotional book called *Twenty-Four Hours a Day* and the *AA Big Book*. I either wanted to change my life or I didn't. I knew if I started my morning off with something uplifting and asked God for help, I may have a chance to make it through the day without drinking or killing myself.

> "*God understands our prayers even when we can't find the words to say them.*"
> —**Author Unknown**

I read from each of these books and used my Franklin Planner to journal the verses and thoughts that inspired me. Then I said a few prayers. The *Our Father*, the *Serenity Prayer*, a *Hail Mary* and I started to just talk to God. It's weird to talk when no one is physically there. *Is anybody even listening*, I would think.

However, I was open to change and I remembered an old verse spoken by Jesus. He said not to repeat the same prayer over and over again. Then he gave an example of a good prayer, which was the *Our Father*. So I was taught as a child to repeat the *Our Father* over and over again. Exactly what Jesus taught people NOT to do! But repeating that was easier and faster than trying to talk to God.

I would say things like, "Good morning God, I don't know what I am doing but if you can help, I hope you will. Help me make it through today. Things aren't looking too good. In fact, things suck! But I'm asking for your help." I didn't know what I was doing but it didn't matter. I was trying to change, which is the beginning of change.

In my morning readings, I especially liked the Psalms of King David. I had a big, red, *Life Application Bible* that gave a little history with the verses as well as explaining some of the verses I didn't understand.

I related to David. For example, Psalm 3:1-2, "O Lord, how many are my foes! How many rise up against me! Many are saying of me, "God will not deliver him." Or Psalm 13:1-2, "How long, O Lord? Will you forget me forever? How long will you hide your face from me? How long must I wrestle with my thoughts and every day have sorrow in my heart? How long will my enemy triumph over me?" After complaining a little, David would then change and make powerful praise such as: "But I trust in your unfailing love; my heart rejoices in your salvation. I will sing to the Lord, for he has been good to me." –Psalm 13:5-6.

This altered my whole perspective. David seemed to get frustrated, would let it out, then praise and thank God. It reminded me of the movie *The Apostle* with Robert Duvall. There is a scene in his bedroom where he was praying but literally yelling at God. Then he becomes humble and says, "OK, OK, whatever you want." (Or something like that). So I decided it was OK to complain to God (cast your cares), but then be humble and say, "Whatever you want." And I meant it.

None of that may be theologically correct, but the point is I was making an effort, was sincere, and theology didn't matter. God met me where I was. After spending some time in morning devotion, it was time to get a shower.

There is a community recreational center in Brentwood, just off of Concord Road that opens at 5 a.m. I started my car and headed down I-65 North towards the center. They charged three dollars to exercise. I figured instead of paying ten dollars for a shower at the truck stop, I'd just go to the rec center to shower every morning.

My Mentor

It had been thirty days since I had my last drink. I slept in my car at night and showered at the rec. center in the morning. When I could find some work I would work and make a couple of dollars. Luckily, I had a tax refund of $1000 that I had been using for expenses. My only expenses were $100 for my storage unit, gas for my car and food. I was also selling my music CDs at a used CD store in Nashville. Life seemed simple without having to pay rent.

I attended two to three meetings a day if I wasn't working. What else was I going to do? In between meetings I hung out at Starbucks, Barnes n Noble, or Costco. Costco was my favorite place because I could get free food samples at lunchtime. If I wanted something more substantial, I could order a drink and a hot dog for $1.50. I kept a blue, plastic box in my backseat with whole-wheat bagels, peanut butter and jelly. This kept my food expenses low. I also kept a plastic jug of water in my car so I never had to buy drinks.

After thirty days I started looking for what they call a "sponsor" or mentor to help me work the twelve steps of the program. It was · tough. There were a lot of crazy people in those meetings, some hadn't had a drink in years but were still running from something. Others added their own rules and ideas to the program. Rules like: don't go anywhere near alcohol, call your sponsor every day, go to 90 meetings in 90 days, don't have sex, never be alone (because then

> *"All life is an experiment.*
> *The more experiments you*
> *make the better."*
>
> **—Ralph Waldo Emerson**

you're alone with a killer, yourself), etc. When I read the Big Book, it didn't say any of this. It talked of a new freedom and power. Yet many people there didn't have much freedom that I could see.

The difference in me at this point was that I was desperately afraid of drinking again. I had no idea how to quit and live at peace long term. The Big Book outlined twelve steps to take and I wanted to take them. *This is my way out*, I thought. "If this doesn't work I can kill myself and look God in the eye and say, 'I tried but you didn't send any help.'" In order to be able to say that to my Creator, though, I had to thoroughly follow the program as outlined in the book. I had to follow it step by step.

Since I had been in and out of a lot of 12-step meetings, I was familiar with the literature. I decided to ignore the things in the meetings that I disagreed with that didn't conform to the book. The book was my textbook. I would follow it, I would follow it to a T and either it would work or it wouldn't. It was like my personal science experiment. I had never really followed through with anything in my life. But I decided I would follow the instructions in the book as if my life depended upon it. And in a way, it did.

The Big Book was written in 1934. It has been used by millions of people to quit drinking and live happy, useful lives. The idea is for someone who has gone through the steps already, to then help a newcomer with the process. He can answer questions and offer his experience of how the principles worked in his life. In searching for a sponsor you are supposed to "find someone that has what you want."

Larry A.

My name is Larry. I'm an alcoholic." He was sitting in the front row of the 12-step meeting wearing tan loafers, khaki pants and a white, collared short sleeve shirt. His hair was dark with shades of gray and combed back. Larry looked a little like former San Francisco 49ers quarterback Joe Montana. He appeared to know everyone and could quote the Big Book and apply its principles to almost any situation. He seemed to truly have a heart to help others, yet was stubborn when it came to doing things differently than the principles of the program as outlined in the Big Book.

Larry spent years and years of his life in and out of hospitals and jail cells. One night on a dark road while driving drunk, he hit another car that was pulling onto the road. A little girl in the other car was killed. Larry went to jail, but continued to drink for another seven years after he got out of prison.

Larry hit rock bottom when he was inside an old log cabin in the middle of the woods. He was dying when he asked his Higher Power for help. He went to a 12-step meeting and never drank again.

When I met him, he had 21 years of sobriety. During those 21 years he had given countless speeches to high school students and policemen on alcoholism and had helped many people gain sobriety and a new life. He faced bankruptcy, illness and the death of loved ones without turning to alcohol. He was totally committed to a spiritual way of life.

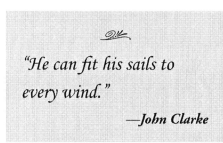

"He can fit his sails to every wind."

—*John Clarke*

Larry had what it took. He followed the book. I was afraid he wouldn't sponsor me since it seemed he worked with several other people already. I asked him anyway. He said yes.

Next to his shiny red pick up truck parked on the street outside of a church he gave me his business card and said, "Call me if you need me. If you don't get me I will always call back." To this day, he always has. He said, "I don't tell my sponsees what to do but I will share my experience at how I've handled similar things in my life. Also, if I haven't had a similar experience I'll tell you how I may handle it using the principles as guides." To this day he has never told me what to do.

In one of our first meetings together, sitting inside his truck, he told me, "Your first thought should be of other people. Selfishness and self-centered fears can drive us to drink. Thinking of how you can best serve others will get you out of self." Talk about life changing advice, that was it for me.

I remember the day I called him and said, "Hey Larry, my third thought was for another person today. That's an improvement because it used to be my fourth thought!" It was true. I made little improvements over time as I tried (and continue) to practice putting others first.

Choose Your Higher Power

One thing that seemed counter-intuitive, yet worked, was the idea of being able to pick my own Higher Power. Higher Power is used in 12-step meetings because many people have pre-conceived notions of God. So at the lowest point of my life, I picked a Higher Power I could relate to.

I grew up Roman Catholic. My family attended mass every Sunday and my parents made financial sacrifices to send me to a private Catholic school. I have the deepest respect for Catholicism but I needed a fresh start.

I chose a loving Creator. One who loves me unconditionally as well as one who lets free will reign on earth. My Creator didn't make me an alcoholic, nor does he allow bad things to happen to teach me a lesson. Sometimes things just happen and many times my life is a reflection of my actions good or bad. It is cause and effect.

Thinking this way freed me from having any resentment towards my Creator to whom I will refer as God. I held onto some of the ideas I grew up with, and some I let go.

For example, I was taught that sex before marriage was a sin. I thought if I sinned I would go to hell. I knew that I wasn't going to wait to be married to have sex, if I could help it. Also, I didn't

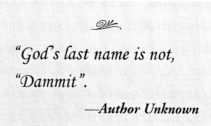

"God's last name is not, "Dammit".

—*Author Unknown*

> *"I know a man who gave up smoking, drinking, sex, and rich food. He was healthy right up to the time he killed himself."*
>
> —*Johnny Carson,*
> *The Tonight Show*

know if I would ever get married. I just wanted to quit drinking, not become a monk. Years earlier I read in Dolly Parton's autobiography that God made sex for us to enjoy, and I agreed. This caused a mild dilemma in my brain. Would having sex outside of marriage as a single man cause me to drink again?

The Big Book is vague on sex relations. However, it does state that I should ask myself, "Is this relationship selfish or not?" Furthermore, we should ask God 'to mold our ideals and help us live up to them.' (p 69, BB) This seemed reasonable to me.

This, for me, meant being honest in my relationships. To tell a woman, "I love you" just to get her naked was selfish and self-centered. Also, running around with married women or telling lies that would hurt someone, including myself, would not fit into my new way of life. This seemed like a reasonable solution that I could work with. However I wasn't sure.

I was still concerned about breaking the rules I was taught as a child. I thought I couldn't be spiritual or give all of myself to God if I was not breaking his rules or doing His Will. Interestingly enough, I wasn't worried about breaking any rules when I was drinking. Yet I had made the decision to change and I had agreed to follow the suggestions in the Big Book to the best of my ability.

Fortunately I found a simple answer through a friend. At a pizza party, I was talking with a lady who had been in the 12-step program for 18 years. Without being specific I told her I was struggling with something that clashes with my concept of Higher Power, my religious upbringing, and the Big Book. She said, "Why don't you just change your concept of a Higher Power?" At that moment I said, "OK." and that was that. Sex before marriage is OK as long as it is not selfish and doesn't hurt anybody. I felt better immediately.

God didn't change. Catholicism didn't change. The Big Book didn't change. My perception changed. Time and time again I found that when my perception changed everything else changed as well. Since so much of what I had perceived in life was causing me to drink, I had to make radical changes in my perception of things and other people.

The principle of changing your concept of a Higher Power is radically different from what I had been told as a child. "God is a vengeful God and he has not changed since the beginning of time." That may or may not be true, I don't know. I will just say that my relationship with God has worked for me. The road does get narrower.

The more I tend to love myself, the less I am seeking love outside of myself. The happier I become with my life, the more protective I become of it. I don't want to let anyone in that can cause me trouble or hurt me down the road. I don't need to be dating or married to be happy. I already am happy. If I am with someone romantically now, it is because I enjoy their company and truly like them.

This was my starting point with God. I needed a concept of a Higher Power to start with. Whatever I had started with, the sun, a tree, a star, or a group of people, would have worked. It was simply a beginning.

With a God I could relate to I now had a Higher Power to ask for help and seek His Will to carry out. This alone would not keep me sober. The illness of addiction centers in the mind. Years of habitual thinking needed to be dealt with and changed. Blaming others, waiting to be rescued from my problems and over dependence on others couldn't be changed overnight. Just like learning how to walk, or ice skate, or ride a bike, there are many falls. That is all part of the learning process. One big obstacle I had to overcome was dealing with the fears I held in my mind.

Dealing with Fear

Every night I'd go back to my car and I'd tell myself that I'm only staying for tonight. I am not staying in this car for eight months or a year, just tonight. I can do that for one night. And that's what I concentrated on. Still my mind would wander into fear.

At times I would start to worry about my future. *How am I ever going to retire? What if I get sick with no health benefits? What if my car breaks down? Will I ever find enough income to support myself?"* These fears would attract more fears. Like a snowball going down hill, they would pile up in my mind. I needed relief from them. I had to learn how to deal with those fears without drinking.

There are three things that I learned to help me deal with my fear.

The first was I had to learn to live one day at a time. I would ask myself, *Are my needs taken care of?* If I had a warm and dry place to sleep (my car) and something to eat (peanut butter & jelly bagels) then I was OK.

It is normal to have some initial fear when the car breaks down one day before rent is due, or when I get sick and have to see a doctor. It is not normal for me to project that since my car is broken, I will not have rent, I then will become homeless and die of starvation next to a dumpster. When I do that I become consumed by fear. I am

> "*Thus, appreciation is the antidote to fear.*"
> —**What Happy People Know,**
> **Dr. Dan Baker**

projecting a negative and disabling the future for myself. There is no power in that.

Instead, by keeping my mind on the solution to a temporary problem and having gratitude for what I have, my fear subsides. I can ask myself, *Do I have what I need to make it through today safely?* Then I can ask someone else for help or pull out a paper and pen and start writing possible solutions.

Larry told me, "Fear blocks out the sunlight of the Spirit. If you're only thinking of yourself you're not thinking of how you can be of service to others." Also,

"I have never seen a brave man. All men are frightened. The more intelligent they are, the more they are frightened. The courageous man is the man who forces himself, in spite of his fear, to carry on."

—**General George Patton**

I realized that no one promised me a tomorrow. People die daily by car wrecks, heart attacks, and senseless accidents. Why worry all day about things and then end up dying that night? I started to realize I ought to just enjoy the day and take care of what I can.

The second thing I learned in dealing with fear is to create a fear inventory. I would write down what I was afraid of, why I was afraid of it, what it affects in me. Was it my self-esteem, finances, relationships or ambitions? Basically it is the same as a fourth step inventory in the Big Book, which I will describe later. I did this inventory specifically to deal with my fears.

Many times I have thought I was afraid of one thing or mad at someone, only to write it down on paper and find two or three other things that were really driving my fears. There is something about putting it on paper that helps me to see it and deal with it.

Problems are not the problem. Everybody has problems at one time or another. It is the actions I take and the solutions I choose that will help me deal with any situation. Really, problems are just opportunities for solutions. So part of dealing with my fears is doing something about them.

In dealing with the fears I have to take action. Larry told me, "Create a past you can live with tomorrow. You shouldn't do anything today that will make you look over your shoulder in fear tomorrow." That means being honest with people, and taking care of the things I need to. Basically, don't create a problem that I'm going to have to fix tomorrow. Great advice!

The third lesson I learned in dealing with fear is to have gratitude. Gratitude is the antidote for fear. I had to learn to find things to be grateful for instead of finding things to complain about.

I had my health, eyesight, hearing, a great singing voice, shoes, intelligence, hands, fingers, a guitar and an opportunity to prosper financially, among many other things. I learned to be grateful for all these things. I was also grateful for my sponsor Larry and all his help.

Everybody should have a Larry A. in their lives, a friend, mentor, and a man I genuinely respect. For six years now I have been able to talk to him about what's going on in my life and get input on how I may handle certain things. Again, he never tells me what to do. He lets me figure things out. However, he does point out things I need to take into consideration. I always listen to what he has to say. He is never judgmental, and always open-minded. I don't think I would have stayed sober long without his help when I first started out. There is another great man that taught me some valuable lessons as well.

Attitude of Gratitude—
A lesson from Father Gordon

A friend invited me to a bible study class attended by other recovering alcoholics. They referred to themselves as "the bloody knees" group; they fall down, then get back up. It was only a couple miles down the road from the truck stop where I slept so I started to attend it every Saturday morning. It was held inside the community center of St. Ignatius Greek Orthodox Church.

St. Ignatius sits off the road several hundred feet, surrounded by gentle rolling hills and pastures. There was a fishing pond in front and a gravel road that led up to the church. The community center had a small wooden deck on the front with a stairway leading up to it. This is where I first met Father Gordon.

Father Gordon wore a black shirt with black pants with a silver cross around his neck. His hair and beard where white. He had a very gentle, soft-spoken manner about him and would smile upon meeting you. Many years ago he was very involved with Campus Crusade for Christ at Ohio State where, I believe, he also taught. His depth of knowledge of the

"Believe your beliefs and doubt your doubts. Think positive, don't start believing the wrong things and doubting the right things."

—*Father Gordon Walker*

> "Appreciation is the highest, purest form of love."
>
> —*What Happy People Know,*
> *Dr. Dan Baker*

scriptures, life experience and open mindedness were extraordinary. I felt I was in the presence of a holy man when I was around him. He could break a complex verse into simple words so even I could understand it. He always spoke with love.

Saturday mornings someone would volunteer to lead the group. That person would choose a bible verse and we would share how we could apply it to our lives. After everyone shared Father Gordon would speak. Sometimes he would answer questions, go into a history lesson, or give a lesson on the scripture. I was glued to his words and took notes to learn and remember as much as I could.

One morning our verse was from 1 Thessalonians 5:16-18: "Be joyful always; pray continually; give thanks in ALL circumstances, for this is God's Will for you in Christ Jesus. Father Gordon suggested that part of God's Will for us, just as the verse states, was to be grateful for ALL things; good and bad. Sometimes bad things turn out good and some good things turn out bad. So we should welcome them all and continually give thanks to God for EVERY situation. Part of faith is to trust God and giving thanks is a way of doing that.

Something inside of me, in that moment, understood. *Life is just a temporary game*, I thought. *I should find something in every situation to be grateful for and then give thanks. It's just a game, and I can be grateful for the bad times because, who knows? They might be the best things that ever happen to me!* Even though I had heard this scripture and sermons on it before, I never really heard the message, "Be thankful for the bad." That never registered with me until that moment.

That night I eased the seat back of my 13-year-old Chrysler New Yorker. I was parked in my usual spot at the back of the Peytonsville Road truck stop. With my eyes closed I prayed, "Thank you God for a . . . (I thought) . . . for a warm and dry place to sleep. Thank you that I am sober. Thank you that if I get cold, all I have to do is start up my car and turn on the heater. Thank you I have a bathroom with running water inside the truck stop. All I have to do is run across the parking lot to get to it! Thank you I never have to clean the toilets." And I meant it.

That Tuesday I didn't have any work, so after showering at the rec. center, I went hiking. Radnor Lake is 1,200 acres park in the middle of Brentwood, an affluent suburb of Nashville. It has an 85-acre lake, along with several miles of hiking trails. It provided solitude and peace for me as I walked its hilly, scenic trails.

As I hiked around the wooded trails to the lake, thinking and dreaming about my future, I came to an opening. There were two empty benches overlooking the serene lake. A few ducks were quacking and swimming in the placid lake. I sat down on a bench to soak up the view as I watched the sun's rays sparkle off the water.

I thought to myself, *If I were Donald Trump I would buy this lake and put a house right here. I would build a big deck and enjoy this view every morning with coffee.* Another thought surfaced, *Maybe I should really buckle down, work two jobs, save every penny and then I could build a house by a lake.* Immediately after that I thought, Why wait 20 years? I have the view right now!

The view of this lake is what I want. Donald Trump has been working hard for thirty years and still is. He doesn't have time to enjoy this view. I do! If he owned this lake he would have to pay taxes, maintenance, utilities, and buy materials just to maintain the house and lake

> *"If I shall sell both my forenoons and afternoons to society, as most appear to do, I am sure that for me there would be nothing left worth living for. I trust that I shall never thus sell my birthright for a mess of pottage."*
>
> —*Thoreau*

> *"Time will take your money, but money won't buy time"*
>
> —*James Taylor*

after he bought it. He would have to continue to work. I don't want the house; I want the view and the time to enjoy it. I have that! Why work twenty years to get what is right in front of me? Who cares who officially owns it? I get to enjoy it right here, right now!"

Wow! My mind started racing. What if I applied that thought to everything? The Donald has to pay taxes for the library in his house. He has to spend money on subscriptions, electricity, water, janitorial services, and employees. The county library has all of those things and it's free! I'm sure the Trump library is spectacular, but I now have a library in Franklin, Brentwood, Nashville, in fact, all over the country. My perspective started to change.

What if I viewed the world as my home? I decided to try that. The highways and roads were my hallways to the different rooms in my home. My kitchen was a whole restaurant. Instead of pulling a belt out of my closet, I had a mall. Thinking of the world as my home started getting fun!

The ceilings in my atrium are . . . limitless! Just look up. That is the ceiling. How about that? Try to heat a home like that. Well, my home is heated. And the furnace has not needed a service call in over four-and-a-half billion years. You ask, "How much is your heating bill?" Uhhh, zero! So, you may be wondering what are the rooms like in this home of mine.

The Donald probably has an impressive gym. Of course, the rec center I use to shower has an Olympic pool, tennis courts (inside and out), weights and cardio equipment, trainers, janitors, and a friendly staff. And they are all working for me, but I don't have to work to pay them. They keep the facility clean, make the coffee, and give me a smile when I enter for only $3. In fact, if I get tired of one, there are two more rec centers within a 30-mile radius. Poor Donald would have to work out alone or with a trainer. My gyms are filled up with friends that I can talk to and look forward to seeing. Trump pays for the whole enchilada, I only pay for what I use.

The best part is my kitchen. Most people have a kitchen and eat meals based on time of day, like breakfast in the morning, or on cuisine, like Italian. Well, since the world is my home, I have a whole restaurant just for pancakes, the Pancake Pantry. Instead of one coffee machine, I have a Starbucks, It's a Grind, Frisky Berry, and countless others scattered all about town. And they all have free Internet and a bathroom! Neither of which I pay for or clean. I just pay for the one single cup of coffee I buy.

Trump's kitchen has to stay stocked with a variety of fresh foods so the chef can make whatever he wants. Everything he wants for a meal has to be ready and on hand. The best fruits and vegetables will spoil if not used timely. So his chef has to replenish everything to make sure it is available. He ends up wasting fruits, vegetables, and dairy products. My restaurants always have fresh fruits and vegetables and I never have to throw out the rotten bananas. That is all taken care of. Usually they are eaten before they go bad by other 'guests' in my home. How lucky can one guy get? Of course, it gets better when I talk about my home.

Bill Gates, co-founder of Microsoft, built a 66,000 square foot home. It took seven years to build, has 24 bathrooms and 6 kitchens. His property taxes in 2009 were $1.063 million dollars!

My home has 5,502,532,127,000,000 square feet! (Which is read, "Five quadrillion, five hundred two trillion, five hundred thirty-two billion, one hundred twenty-seven million square feet", or just "Five-and-a-half quadrillion" for short.)* It has taken approximately 4.55 billion years to build my home, and it is still under construction.

In Franklin alone I have way more than 24 bathrooms. I have more kitchens, several for each cuisine, and my property tax liability is—let me see, zero times zero, carry the zero equals . . . Zero!

Instead of a sunroom, I have California!

With gratitude and my newfound perspective I found myself to be the richest man in the world! After all, my home is the biggest in the world. It is the world. What mattered more to me was time.

I had the same twenty-four hours a day others have but I wasn't working sixty or eighty hours a week. I had the time to go hiking, sip a cup of coffee at Barnes n Noble, or get free food samples at Costco. I worked for twenty years doing work I didn't love to pay for a home I couldn't afford. Previously I was broke in time and money. Now I decided to be rich in time and, temporarily, poor in money. Instead of zero for two, I was now one for two, and that was a big improvement. For the first time in my life, time became more important than money.

"Everything is an Inventory!"

There were reasons why I drank. On the surface and deep inside me were resentments, angers and fears. If I was to stay sober I had to get these out in the open and deal with them instead of keeping them inside. To do this, I had to take inventory.

Larry would say: "When we act upon our defects of character, our guilt, anger and fear, we become restless, irritable and discontent. We block out the Sunlight of the Spirit and go back to drinking and our selfish ways. If we take inventory of our defects of character and carry the principles of the 12-step program into our lives we will have peace of mind and will not want to take a drink. We can then put others first and think of how we may best serve others, instead of thinking only about ourselves all the time, as we used to."

As part of the 12-step process I had to write down all my resentments and fears on a piece of paper. This is a four-column exercise. People, places and institutions that I was angry with were listed in the first column. The second column listed the reasons behind the anger. The third was what part of me this fear or resentment affected: my security, self-esteem, ego, sex relations, or fears. And lastly, I was to write what my responsibility was in the issue at hand.

This process is called the Fourth Step

> *"When resentful thoughts come, try to pause and count your blessings."*
>
> —*p. 119 Alcoholics Anonymous*

> *"Action is a great restorer and builder of confidence. Inaction is not only the result, but the cause, of fear. Perhaps the action you take will be successful: perhaps different action or adjustments will have to follow. But any action is better than no action at all."*
>
> —**Norman Vincent Peale**

inventory. I made it a goal to have it completed by the end of April. I procrastinated for several weeks, then thought, *If I don't do this, I think I'll go back to drinking.* This was a good dose of fear for me so I scheduled two hours on the next two Saturdays to go to the Brentwood Public Library and work on my list.

I had tried this process before but only came up with a few items. This time I wanted to be thorough, as though my life depended on it. I felt it did. I grabbed a desk in a corner of the library away from everybody. Then I said a prayer and followed the instructions, step by step, in the Big Book of AA. Sentence by sentence I read and then wrote down what the book asked me to do. When I finished writing I checked off that sentence and went to the next sentence. I only brought two sheets of paper so I had to go to the copy machine in the library and grab, or steal, a couple more sheets of paper. Hey, that paper is there for public use, right?

I was surprised at how much I wrote. Something inside of me opened up and I just wrote whatever I thought without considering if it should be there or not. I figured my sponsor could sort through what should and shouldn't be there.

The second Saturday I finished the inventory. I asked God to help me think of anything I may have missed but nothing came to mind.

Looking at the inventory in black and white, I realized that in almost every situation I either started my troubles or I pushed back when someone started with me. All my life I thought I was the good guy. Like Curly in the Three Stogies would say, "I'm a victim of circumstance." The inventory told me differently.

In a previous job, I felt my boss wronged me. I had worked hard for a promotion putting in extra time and effort to get the position. He never gave me the promotion. I felt I earned it and he was doing it to spite me. I literally ignored him for six months. I would walk into a meeting and say hello to everyone except him. I would not look at or say hello to him when we passed in the hallway. This kind of attitude caused more problems for me on this job. Eventually, I quit because of what they were supposedly doing to me. In reality, no company can survive with an employee that gets drunk on the job, shows up late, doesn't take responsibility, and ignores its leadership. I was the reason for my job troubles, not my boss.

I resented and blamed my parents for my life not turning out the way I wanted it to. At that time, I had been living on my own for 16 years. Growing up, my parents provided a loving home, education, a solid work ethic, a spiritual upbringing, food, shelter, and everything I needed to succeed in life. It wasn't them; it was me. I had to accept responsibility for where I was in life. I had 21 years of opportunity with them and 16 years on my own to work towards whatever I wanted to attain in life. Instead I fell into self-pity, blaming others, and I got drunk.

Looking at the fourth column of this list it became clear that I got what I deserved in life. Life is cause and effect. Each action brings about an effect. If I act bitter, hostile and resentful to others and the world at large, I will get that in return. I simply could not become useful if I con-

> *"The first principle of success I that you should never be angry."*
> —*p. 111 Alcoholics Anonymous*

tinued this way. I had big changes to make if I wanted to be happy, joyous and free in life.

For many years of my life I have read books about positive thinking. They contain many basic principles that are proven time and again. Unfortunately, I never applied them without wanting something in return. I expected fame and fortune to come instantly. I was only thinking of myself when I read those books. I thought of how great I could be instead of thinking of how I could use those principles to make myself useful to others. Since I never received the instantaneous results I wanted after reading these books I would seldom adopt the principles as part of my behavior on a daily basis.

The things I wanted in life were extreme. I wanted to be a rock star. I wanted women to want me and men to fear me. I wanted a private jet, a mansion and a limo. It is tough to be content in life when your desires are that of a 12-year-old child.

Much of my behavior was also based on unrealistic fears. Fear I would become a nobody and fear I would never be enough. Fear of people not respecting me nor thinking twice about me. Fear of losing everything I had. And my fears centered around me. Me, me, me. I learned that any concern I had for another person had to do with getting something I wanted. In the end I was just an egomaniac with an inferiority complex.

Some of my fears became a reality. The good thing about losing everything is I no longer had to fear losing it. I learned it really wasn't that big of a deal. Other fears just needed to be dealt with in an adult manner.

This inventory helped me learn how to deal with my fears. In the serenity prayer it says, "God, grant me the serenity to accept the things I cannot change, the courage to change the things I can, and the wisdom to know the difference." It is a self-fulfilling prayer. If I can do something about a situation, than I am to take action. If not, I still take an action. The action is to ask God for serenity to accept a situation I have no control over. It's that simple. Then, it is time to see how I can be of service to others. I must move on from situation to situation and change what I can, and accept what I cannot change. This principle is simple and effective and has helped me overcome many obstacles in my path without resorting to the bottle.

On the third Saturday I sat inside Larry's red pickup truck after a meeting while the rain came down in big, heavy drops. With the truck

> *"So often in time it happens, we all live our life in chains, and we never even know we have the key".*
> —**Already Gone, The Eagles**

running and his windshield wipers cleaning the windshield, I read him my list. He listened intently. Sometimes he laughed and said, "Yep, I did the same thing!" I was afraid of sharing this list with anyone except Larry. At this point he had earned my complete trust. I trusted he would keep this confidential between us and he wouldn't laugh at me or make me feel bad. I was right. Larry was knowledgeable, experienced and compassionate. The purpose of this step was for me to share all my secrets with another person. It was to give me some humility.

I finished reading my list to Larry, we said a prayer and I left. Later that day I reviewed everything I had done up to that point. I had completed steps 1 through 5 in the 12-step process. I concluded that I had done everything honestly and to the best of my ability. I heard people say that at this point they have some kind of emotional experience and they cry. I didn't, not yet.

The next morning was Sunday. I had been working and sleeping back at my friend Fred's winery again, where I had previously stayed. They needed help planting grapes, mowing and maintaining the property. Fred and some investors bought an additional 25 acres of land that had another farmhouse on it. I was offered the temporary use of that farmhouse along with ten dollars an hour pay for my labor. I could stay in the house until they decided to start construction on it to turn the house into offices and a tasting room. (I ended up sleeping there for 7 weeks!)

I woke up that morning, grabbed my books, walked out of the

house and up to the top of the hill located on the winery acreage. The sun was starting to peek out from behind a leafy green hill on the horizon. Birds were singing and a light fog settled on the fields below. I read my devotional books and some Psalms. As I breathed in the cool spring air, I said a quick prayer. Then I broke down. Tears of gratitude and shame were mixed together. I was ashamed of my old life but grateful for over three months of sobriety and how my life was coming together.

Growing up watching John Wayne and Clint Eastwood movies I always felt a man shouldn't cry. In the movie, *The Outlaw Jose Wales*, Clint Eastwood spits tobacco on the forehead of a dead outlaw. Someone asks him if they should bury the man and Clint says, "Worms gotta eat. Buzzards too." I always wanted to be that kind of tough guy. I wanted to be super cool, walking around kicking ass and taking names. Once again I was an adult with childish ideas on how to live life.

I had to let go of the idea that real men don't cry. I was going through a cleansing process and I needed to let it all out, good and bad. I was just a man on a country hill at dawn going through this process of healing and change.

A big part of going through the life-changing process is having hope that things will get better. After years of bombarding my mind with negative thoughts and expectations, I needed to intentionally change the way I thought. If I caught myself thinking a negative, angry, or hurtful thought, I deliberately willed myself to change it. I would say a prayer and think an optimistic thought. That may be too simple for some people, but it worked for me. My sponsor Larry helped me with this as well.

Positive Expectations

After working on the 12-step program with Larry for eight months, still living out of my car, I called him up one day. I was at the laundromat doing laundry. It was a beautiful, bright, sunny day. I said, "Hey Larry." Larry responded, "Hey Mr. Dan, how are you?" (Dan is my real name; Sutton is a nickname). "I'm doing great, Larry! I'm having a good day today, I had a good day yesterday, in fact I've had good days for the last couple of weeks! But that will change," I exclaimed in sort of a joking way. Larry retorted, "Now why in the hell would you say a thing like that?"

"Well," I replied sheepishly, "I heard in a meeting that 'this too shall pass', and the people said if they were having bad days, they know it would pass, and if they were having good days, this too shall pass."

"Ahhh, that's bullshit!" Larry exclaimed. "You should wake up everyday with a positive expectation for that day. You should have a positive mindset and expect good things to happen. Why would you ever want to expect good things to pass? Don't listen to those people in the meetings who are negative."

This sounded like good advice to me. It is much more fun to start off my day expecting good things to happen as well.

> "By trying we can easily learn to endure adversity. Another man's, I mean."
>
> —*Mark Twain*

JOURNAL STORIES

I kept a journal that first year in my car. Below are just a few lessons I learned.

JOURNAL ENTRY

Friday, March 18th 2005

God Will Take Care of Me

This morning I had a negative $30 in the bank. 55 cents in change in my car and three quarters of a tank of gas and no food and one pass left to the gym where I showered. I was frustrated. I've looked for work this week, I've already sold the majority of my CDs for money which is gone. I prayed, meditated, read psalm 13 and remembered god promised to take care of me like the lilies in the field and the birds in the air. I figured I could go without food for a couple of days if need be. Before I left the gym Mandy Green who works there encouraged me, gave me $5, yogurt, cheese, and an orange juice. God took care of me, no need to worry even though sometimes I still do he loves me.

I woke up at the truck stop. I was afraid. I had a negative $30 in the bank, fifty-five cents in change inside my car, three-quarters of a tank of gas, no food and one pass left to the rec center. Most of the CDs I was selling were gone. I knew I was up against it. I was in fear.

> "I hated every minute of training, but I said, "Don't quit. Suffer now and live the rest of your life as a champion."
>
> —*Muhammad Ali*

I briefly meditated, then read Psalm 13. That morning I remembered an old verse in the Bible. It read something like: I take care of the lilies in the field and the birds in the air and I will take care of you.

So I prayed, "God, you said you would take care of me like the lilies in the field and the birds in the air. Well, now is a good time to start. I'm down to nothing. I'm not trying to test you but I REALLY need some help. If you're going to take care of me, as you say you are, today is a good day to start."

I felt that this day was a test. Not that I believe God tests me, but this was a situation I had to deal with nonetheless and exercise what faith I had.

I started up my car and drove to the rec center to shower. On the way in I spoke with my friend Mandy who works there. Mandy was a wonderful woman who always had a smile and a word of encouragement for me. She knew I was living in my car and never looked down upon me for it. I briefly shared that I was up against it but I had faith something would come through if I just kept doing the next right thing.

After a workout and shower I grabbed my gym bag and headed out the door. As I walked down the hallway of the rec center I said goodbye to Mandy. She called me over. Then she gave me five dollars, a yogurt, a stick of cheese and an orange juice. She said, "I know this isn't much but I hope it helps you."

People can call this a coincidence. Some call it "coinci-God." I felt it was a small miracle. I started the day with no way of knowing how I could make it through and I asked God for help. Help came in the form of Mandy's gift to me. She knew I wasn't asking her for help or feeling sorry for myself when we talked earlier. We were just two friends talking.

I believe sometimes miracles happen in such an ordinary way that after they happen they are easy to dismiss.

I walked out of the rec center, got into my car and cried. This, for me, was an answer from God. He would take care of me. It wasn't the lottery; it was "my daily bread." And that is all I needed.

Several days later I was in the same situation. In a meeting I spoke up and said, "Even though I am out of work and looking, I believe God will take care of me." After I finished speaking, a man I had never seen before motioned that he wanted to speak with me after the meeting. He later told me that the contractor painting his house has a job opening and he would be willing to pass my number to him. I got the job.

From this I learned that I needed to be less self-sufficient and more willing to share my struggles. Other people are willing to help and offer opportunities if they know I need it. If I keep everything to myself, though, I am denying them a chance to help and denying myself help when I need it.

April 11th, 2005

Being Grateful When I Don't Mean It

A tough day today. I had to weed eat several ditches. I was wore out. I wanted to quit. I prayed and cursed. Stones kept kicking up and hitting me in the face. Ten years ago I moved here to Nashville and made $8.50 to start work inside an air-conditioned, clean office. Now I make $8 busting my ass; dangerous work. I start painting for Randy on Friday for $9. I told Daryll I would help him through Thursday and I will. I don't take lunch yet a half hour has been subtracted lately from my pay for lunch every day. I need to learn humility, hard work, discipline and persistence. I am learning that sometimes kicking and screaming but I am learning. This too shall pass.

It is easy to be grateful when things are going well, but this particular day really put me to the test. My weight was hovering around 245 lbs., a good 50 lbs. overweight for someone 6 feet tall. I was mowing yards for $8/hr, mainly running the weed trimmer.

After starting at 7 a.m., I was getting pretty tired by the early afternoon. It was the first warm day of spring and the sun seemed to blast its rays onto my freckled, white skin, which responded by turning beet red. We had already finished several yards with me running the weed trimmer. Walking and swinging the strapless machine up and down hills, around trees and shrubs, wore me out. On this day though, those yards were only warm ups for the VFW post.

It was a yellow-stained, cinder-blocked building with a gravel parking lot and stones scattered about the yard. The drainage ditch ran parallel to the road. This was our first mowing of the year of this particular property, which translates to: "The grass is high!"

The drainage ditch was too much for me. It was no ordinary ditch, it was the alpha ditch. It was about ten feet deep from the road and ran parallel to the front road. I would try navigate the steep embankment with each step while swinging the buzzing weed trimmer against the tall, damp grass. My foot would slide out from underneath me and the weed trimmer would rocket into the sky and my butt would kiss the earth. Each time I would cuss. I was pissed off!

I decided to reach out to God for help. My conversation with God went like this, "God, you created the Milky Way, all of the galaxies, the earth, all life on it; you delivered me from my drinking and this is the best you can do with my life? $8 an hour? I'm in my car, Lord, I can never afford an apartment on $8 an hour. So now I'm doing something I hate, I'm tired, my bones ache, I'll probably lose an eye or get hurt. I have no insurance. The best I can do tonight is take a shower somewhere and sleep in my car. Is this your plan for the rest of my life? Is this the best you can do for me? If this is your plan, God, then it sucks. Go ahead and hit me with lightening, it would be a relief. I'm not scared of dying, go ahead, please. If this is all I have to look forward to in life then I'd rather be dead."

All the while my weed trimmer would hit the little stones that were scattered about the yard and sling shot them into my face. That did it! I was going to quit. I would just lay the weed trimmer down and walk

"Space ain't man's final frontier, man's final frontier is the soul".
—Man's Final Frontier, Arrested Development

the ten miles back to my car. I was broke and homeless and this job is not going to change that for me. If I quit I can be broke and homeless without having to expose myself to injury and frustration.

I stopped and thought for a minute. *What have I learned?* I asked myself.

"Be grateful for all things, good and bad." "Give notice before quitting a job." and "Never leave one job until you have another."

As I paused I said the serenity prayer, "God, grant me the serenity to accept the things I cannot change, the courage to change the things I can, and the wisdom to know the difference." I thanked God for my job and the opportunity he has provided to me. Then I pulled the starter cord to the weed trimmer and continued cutting grass. Shortly after I resumed another stone stung the side of my face. "Motherf****, G**dam***, S**of******!" Then I said the serenity prayer, again and again. After that I thanked God and I laughed.

I pictured God looking down on me with a grin. He knew, and I knew, I was not one bit thankful for anything at that point. In fact I was being sarcastic. I would pray, "Thank you God, heavenly Father, for this job. You are a genius! What a great plan you have for me, I'm so glad I quit drinking and turned my will over to you. I could have never thought of a better plan for my life. Impressive, God." I wanted to be sincere but I really wasn't thankful at all. I was just going through the motions.

Then I started laughing and I pictured God laughing with me. God knew I was lying! I knew I was lying. But I was being obedient. I was giving gratitude; at least I was trying to! That was a big improvement for me. I hated weed trimming that yard, but I tried to be thankful and obedient the best way I could.

Then I would get a little more serious, "God, I am thankful I have a job that makes me money so I can eat and buy gas and I know something better will come along if I continue to be faithful, this is kind of a test." Then a pebble would pelt my cheek like a BB gun, and the whole process would repeat itself. "Moth********, g********". You get the point.

I made it through the workday without quitting or getting hurt.

Later that night I was with some friends and we all laughed as I told them the process of getting hit, swearing, praying, thanking, then getting hit again, swearing….

Once again I learned that God will meet me wherever I am if I just reach out to him. There is a famous poem called, "Footprints," which talks of God carrying the author at times. I don't refute that that was his experience. But my experience was a little different.

Sometimes there is one set of footprints because God is walking over to me. If I am separated from God, I don't have to move the entire distance back to him. God will come over to me. I do have to reach out to God and walk. God won't carry me. He has given me talents, abilities and gifts that he wants me to use, learn to use and develop. For me, reliance on God also means having enough faith to do something, even if only to do it poorly. God needs some level of cooperation from me. I have free will to turn my back on him or reach out to him.

JOURNAL ENTRY

Friday July 1st 2005

Change Is Gonna Come

A tiring day. Played out (music) last night until 2am. Got home at 2:30. Slept until 8:30am, started work at 11 due to rain. Only worked three hours. Found out we have a last second gig at the pub. Took a nap. Fred called and said I had to be out of the house by Monday due to renovations. Homeless again, let's see what God can do this time.

After living on the Vineyard for 7 weeks during the summer, I had to move again. I was run down and tired. Too tired to be frustrated. At that time it seemed like I would build my sand castle then someone would come and kick it down.

But I was OK with this for two reasons. Before moving into the farmhouse on the winery I did an inventory of the situation: Pros, and Cons. I thought about what might happen and knew there would always be an unknown element to any situation.

The Pros would be:
- I have a place to stay.
- It is close to work (at work).
- I will have a free shower.
- There is no rent.

- It is on a beautiful farm.
- It is safe.
- I will be able to sleep much better.
- I will have access to a kitchen.

Cons:
- It is only temporary (of course, so what?).
- I am liable for any damage or accidents (Unlikely. They were going to gut the house to remodel it, so I couldn't damage it, not that I would anyway. So, basically, unless a freak accident or fire happened, I would be fine.)

Really there were no cons. Some people in my 12-step group mentioned it was on a winery but I wasn't going there to drink. They weren't even making wine yet. It was just a grape farm at that time, and besides, if someone is working the program they should be able to go anywhere and do anything a non-alcoholic person could.

I knew it was temporary housing when I moved in. I was fine with moving again partly because I had I completed an inventory of the situation before I made the decision to move.

I had complete gratitude for being able to stay in that house and knew each night was a gift. I felt that living in my car was what I had earned and being able to sleep on the bedroom floor of an air-conditioned house with a shower was more than I deserved. I was willing to pay whatever price I had to pay but if a gift like the farmhouse came along, I was humble enough to accept it.

Life is tough enough as it is. I've been too proud at times in my life to accept help. I needed to learn to accept help with humility, also knowing that accepting a gift is a gift back to the person that gives it.

I could have been fearful and angry because I had to move out of the farmhouse, but I wasn't. I trusted God, had gratitude and was willing to pay whatever price I had to pay.

What happened? I moved from the floor of a farmhouse to the bed of a million dollar home with an in-ground pool! Yes, this was a temporary job, house-sitting for Fred while his family went on vacation.

Everything is temporary in life. It's just one day at a time. I had no guarantee for tomorrow. So I lived in the day. And for those ten days when I was house-sitting, I lived like a millionaire!

This was even better than a millionaire because I didn't have to work for any of it. I didn't have to pay property tax, a water bill, a heating bill, a landscaping service, housecleaner, etc. I didn't have to work overtime, sit in boring meetings, or travel to places I didn't want to go to meet people I didn't want to meet. I just had to take care of the two dogs and watch over everything. I could use the kitchen and I was invited to help myself to the food - which I did, of course!

Solomon says, "So I commend the enjoyment of life, because nothing is better for a man under the sun than to eat and drink and be glad. Then joy will accompany him in his work all the days of the life God has given him under the sun." Ecclesiastes 8:15. I didn't drink but I did get a nice tan lying by the pool!

The first night back in my car after living in this beautiful home I had yet another blessing. My seat was all the way back and I was trying to go to sleep. I looked up through my sunroof and watched the clouds pass over the fluorescent white, full moon. I thought, "My friend in his million dollar home doesn't even have the incredible view from his bed that I have right now. Thank you, God!" Finding gratitude is a beautiful thing.

"It's been too hard living, but I'm afraid to die.
Cause I don't know what's up there beyond the sky.
It's been a long, a long time coming
But I know, a change gonna come, oh yes it will"

—Change is Gonna Come, Sam Cooke

JOURNAL ENTRY

Thursday June 2nd 2005

A crazy day today. My check didn't come in from last Friday. I was getting low on cash. I had taken $80 worth of books back to Borders out of $144. I decided that wasn't good stewardship after talking to my sponsor. I had trouble praying without getting mad about that check. It never came in the mail. I decided to move $200 from my savings into my checking and not worry about it. Everything today seemed to be a test for me. The car wouldn't start. Beautiful girl in a tiny dress at the bank wouldn't pay attention to me. Got cut off in traffic and some personal problems in the band (80's rock band I sang in). I even locked my keys in the car. Luckily a couple of months ago I had a spare key made and had it taped to the bottom of my car. Manageability. Something's were managed, some were out of my control. Disappointing day and all but I am sober and content.

JOURNAL ENTRY

July 15th 2005

Back in my car at the truck stop. They're going to renovate the farm house so I had to move out. I had been putting 10% in the savings and paying my parents off. I have fallen into sloth. I hadn't washed or cleaned my car until today. I've slipped on some things a little so now I have an opportunity to pick things back up. Been playing about three times a week, awesome! And we're playing at a party in September that should have Rascall Flats and a Playboy Playmate in attendance, life is good.

Being intentional in my living helped me to catch myself before I got too sloppy with my habits. Bad habits start as small cobwebs and end up as steel cables that are difficult to break if they are not nipped in the bud.

JOURNAL ENTRY

Friday July 22nd 2005

I'm a bit frustrated. I'm back living in my car, tired, alone, and it seems the only women attracted to me are crazy or ugly. I'm not too spiritual right now. I have the "poor-mes." I do wonder if this life with God doesn't seem too impressive. I guess it is a lot better than it was except the living conditions. I'm playing music and working a job I enjoy and have enough cash and I am losing weight and getting healthier, saving money and giving a lot of money away. I guess it boils down to not having a good woman in my life.

There is a saying, "Poor me, poor me, pour me another drink." It takes a lot of faith to expect a woman to date you when you're living in your car. Perhaps my expectations were too high. Reading this, however, I see where I start looking at the good in my life. Sometimes, I have found, it is OK to complain once and let it out. Then it is time to move on to something more productive.

Also, I had to learn to accept loneliness. It is OK, once in a while, to feel lonely. But usually I am tired or hungry during those times and that intensifies my feelings. There is a formula: HALT. Anytime I am Hungry, Angry, Lonely or Tired, I need to be careful with my emotions and thinking. It is easy for me to get moody under those conditions. Sometimes I just need a nap and a meal and I am fine.

JOURNAL ENTRY

Tuesday September 6th 2005

What a shitty day. The work at the vineyard has dried up and I'm down to my last $50. Also it looks like we may not be playing (music) out at Marathon's on Saturday, he double booked us (booked two bands for one night). I needed that money. Back to the basics. Life kind of sucks. I guess it's time to start a f***ing gratitude list again.

Life is not always kicks and giggles. I often got frustrated, but I would never stay there very long. Even though I was complaining, I knew the solution was to write a gratitude list. I also learned a couple of lessons from this experience.

When working a seasonal job, it is always good to realize it is ***seasonal*** and start looking for work ***before*** the season ends. It's common sense, but being proactive was something I needed to improve upon.

The second lesson here has to do with Murphy's Law. If I'm relying on one gig, or one paycheck to get by, most likely it will cancel or not show up. The Boy Scout motto is: Be Prepared. That is a good motto for daily life, too. Anything can happen. You're booked to mow lawns all day and it rains. You're relying on a Saturday gig to pay Monday's rent and the bar is closed by the state for not paying their sales tax. Those things are out of my control. What is in my control is having some savings, just in case. That also helps to give me peace of mind.

JOURNAL ENTRY

Friday October 14th 2005

Good gig tonight I tried my best. My voice was a little week but it came through on Gloria and Don't Get Fooled Again. I live today and that's what counts for me. Saturday, last week, I played at a doctor's office at the prestigious governor's club, a 7-8000 square foot million dollar home. The doctor looked young and was in his forties. The next day I was at the Embassy vacuuming a volume that had a 20th year high school reunion. The sign said class of 1985. I graduated high school 20 years ago in 1985. My old friends are college professors, home builders and very successful. I'm a homeless musician setting up banquets at a hotel, I'm a loser. Sunday night I decided to do something about it. I ran 5 miles, ran again Monday, Tuesday, I rested Wednesday, ran Thursday and Friday, I want to live everyday like a winner, maybe then I'll be a winner. But if not at least I gave it my best shot. Win or burnout trying. Every day act like a winner. What would a winner do today?

That night I was vacuuming all the confetti off the banquet floor when I saw the sign, "Welcome Class of 1985". I couldn't believe it had been twenty years. I folded the tables and the chairs inside the room. Then I emptied all of the half-filled wine glasses and beer bottles that were left into a 55-gallon, plastic garbage can to be disposed of. They had a party and went home to their families. I worked and then drove to the truck stop to sleep that night.

> "Expectation is the root of all heartache."
> —William Shakespeare

They went to college, worked hard, got married and had families. I drank and raised hell. I never wanted to be in that situation again. I never wanted to be the failure in the group. At that moment I wanted to fight, succeed and stand tall.

I wasn't indulging in self-pity, but I was disappointed in how my life turned out. A fire was ignited inside of me. I hated where I was and knew only I could change my life. Life is cause and effect.

Facts are facts. In high school I would have never dreamed that twenty years later I would be living in my car. NEVER. I had to own up to my choices in life.

Shortly after this, a friend in the 12-step program was looking for a roommate and he asked me if I wanted to move in! That became my first permanent residence in 9 months.

JOURNAL ENTRY

Sunday November 20th 2005

I think I've been able to trace the root of my hatred towards corporate managers. In part it might be my old man bitching about General Motors but a bigger part would be Sonoco Fibre Drum, dealing with supervisor Charlie and being on the safety committee writing up another supervisor and it being turned down even though I proved myself right.

I was working part time at the Embassy Suites in Cool Springs. My job was to set up tables and chairs for the banquets they hosted in the conference rooms. My boss, a likeable man from the Caribbean named Fitz was very detail-oriented. One time I just finished setting up 300 chairs in a room. He came in and the chairs were not lined up to his liking. He picked one up, moved it an inch or two, then told me move all of the chairs so they lined up with the one he moved. Immediately I got pissed off! The 12-step literature instructs me to "pause when agitated". My normal reaction would be to verbally respond in a negative way to my boss's new orders. Thankfully, I paused. While pausing, I said the serenity prayer.

I then thought: *Hey, I like my boss. And I'm getting paid by the hour. What do I care if he wants me to move every chair again? If that's the way he wants it, that's what I will do. He's the boss, and they're paying me.* All that in just a split second! I said, "OK", and went to work. I wondered why I automatically reacted so angrily.

Lying in bed that night, I thought about how mad I got. As I thought about my life, I remembered a time 13 years earlier when I had a confrontation with my boss at the factory and I walked off the job. I really wanted to physically hurt this guy, but I didn't want to go to jail for doing it. I just left. That was it!

I was never one to enjoy authority figures, but I was still pissed off at that boss from 13 years ago! I asked God to help me let go of my resentment and prayed for my old boss and gave thanks for my new boss. Immediately I felt relief. The next day I talked it over with my sponsor and prayed again. That is how it worked for me. Find a problem and work the solution.

JOURNAL ENTRY

January 8th 2006

Sometimes turning points are beginnings. As when I decide to start praising instead of condemning. At other times turning points are endings, such as when I see clearly the need to stop festering resentments or crippling self-seeking.

"When you stop drinking, you have to deal with this marvelous personality that started you drinking in the first place."

—*Jimmy Breslin*

JOURNAL ENTRY

Wednesday February 1st 2006

I got my year chip today. No alcohol for one year. First time in 25 years for that. I'm playing music, living in an apartment, have money in the bank, spend time with pretty women, work a part time job and try to be of service to my fellows. My life has turned around 360 degrees in a year. I've lost 30 pounds. I have good relations with family and have good friends. Praise God I feel healthy. My house is being put in order. Life is good!

"Absolute sunshine breeds a desert."

—Anonymous

SIX YEARS LATER: LOOKING BACK

September, 2010

It was a perfect night for a run. The sun was partially below the horizon as the earth cooled to a refreshing 77 degrees. This was my 91st consecutive day of running at least thirty minutes, and I wasn't going to miss it just because I dumped cookies, cheese, and ice cream into my stomach earlier in the day and felt tired.

One by one the stars began to flicker as the light blue skyline slipped into darkness. I had on my dark blue shirt with bold white lettering on it spelling "Penn State."

Three miles down and I felt good. My horrible eating habits of the day gave me heartburn during my run, but it eased a little after the third mile. When I closed in on my apartment complex, I turned right instead of left. I felt like running more. One mile up the two-lane road the sidewalk ended, so I ran on the street. Up one hill and down another. As I left the street lights and sidewalks were behind me, the moon cast shadows from above. Giant trees lined the left side of the dark road and a quiet cornfield rested my right. My solitude grew with every step I took further from town.

> *"The brave may not live forever, but the cautious do not live at all"*
>
> —*Richard Branson*

> *"You can do anything you set your mind to man."*
> —*Lose Yourself, Eminem*

I turned onto a remote country road and started running down the two mile, descending hill. Green vines covered the lime stonewalls that lined both sides of the narrow road, protecting the sow bean fields from intrusion by motor vehicle. I listened to the sound of the crickets and my running shoes hitting the pavement. My eyes fixed on the yellow moon and the white stars that covered the sky. I felt my breath. Rythmic, calm; like a machine.

I pulled my iPhone out of my pocket to see how far I had run. Six miles, and I felt good. Good enough to try a 13.3 mile, half marathon. No water or food, just a spur of the moment decision to run farther than I ever had to test myself, to see if I could. Somehow I knew I could do it, and I was going to keep on running. Something buried deep inside me, a feeling I prefer to keep to myself, filled my soul and body with a wave of determination. "I will finish this run, even if it kills me, 'cause I should already be dead! I won't be stopped tonight!"

Ah, how easy it can be for me to forget that my life is just bonus hockey. You go to a hockey game, you pay for three twenty-minute periods of hockey, and if the score is tied at the end of those three periods, they keep playing hockey, no extra charge to you. Bonus hockey. But for me, it is different. I tried to kill myself and lived. I lost every material possession I had, and I realized it was no big deal. Most of it was stuff I didn't even need. Yes, each day is like extra whipped cream on a hot fudge sundae. No risk can beat me because I have already lost everything. Because I have nothing to lose, I have already won. Since I should be dead, this life is just a dream.

Have you ever tried to manipulate a dream, once you realized it was a dream? That is my life. I'm just trying some things I was too afraid to try when it seemed to matter. Now, it doesn't matter; a dead man has nothing to lose.

That idea was going through my mind as I raced down the backwoods Tennessee country road lit only by the sliver of moon above.

I held back a couple of tears as I thought about that October morning in 2004. A smile welled up in my heart and touched my face as I thought of that Peggy Lee song again, "If that's all there is, my friend, then let's keep dancing."

"*As we express our gratitude, we must never forget that the highest appreciation is not to utter words, but to live by them*"

—*John F. Kennedy*